Teamworking skills for social workers

Ruben Martin

Open University Press

Open University Press
McGraw-Hill Education
McGraw-Hill House
Shoppenhangers Road
Maidenhead
Berkshire
England
SL6 2QL

email: enquiries@openup.co.uk
world wide web: www.openup.co.uk

and Two Penn Plaza, New York, NY 10121-2289, USA

First published 2013

A catalogue record of this book is available from the British Library

ISBN-13: 978-0-33-524605-2 (pb)
ISBN-10: 0-33-524605-2 (pb)
eISBN: 978-0-33-524648-9

Library of Congress Cataloging-in-Publication Data
CIP data applied for

Typesetting and e-book compilations by
RefineCatch Limited, Bungay, Suffolk

Teamworking skills
for social workers

For my wife, Kay
Let me count the ways

Praise for this book

"At a time when social workers are being castigated for failures in team-working in recent child abuse enquiries, this book is extremely timely. I am not aware of a similar book which is able to convey the basic tenets of team-working as well as the necessary skills to do team working well. It is an important book which should be on the course lists of all early stage social workers.

The book brings together social work theory relating to team work within an ecological framework. Students are given activities to reflect on their current level of skills. Excellent case studies illustrate the issues. The book is totally up-to-date, linking into recent material from the College of Social Work.

I strongly recommend this book. I think students will find the material engaging and accessible, but they will also learn much about the essential team working skills for social work."

Ann Buchanan, Emeritus Professor of Social Work, University of Oxford, UK

"This is a very readable and informative text on an essential element of social work practice. As the author says, social workers do not work autonomously but in teams, whether social work or multidisciplinary. The theoretical base is clearly presented and it is useful to reflect on unconscious processes in teams and organisations. I highly recommend it to practitioners, students and academics."

Joyce Lishman, Professor Emeritus, Robert Gordon University, Aberdeen, UK

"All social workers practise in teams of some description, yet there is little literature to guide that teamwork. This book fills that gap, whilst at once being theoretically informed and accessible. It is a book that can be read through as a whole or dipped into according to need. As such, it will be appreciated by busy practitioners as well as students of social work."

Professor Jonathan Parker, Bournemouth University, UK

"Good social workers develop very personal and private relationships with service users. But they also usually work in teams. Ruben Martin's book blends familiar and contemporary insights on how teams work, but with the focus very clearly on the specific roles and tasks of social care practitioners."

David Shemmings, Visiting Professor of Child Protection Research at Royal Holloway, University of London, UK

Contents

Acknowledgements   xi

PART 1
Overview of teamworking   1

1 **Introduction**   3

2 **What is teamwork and why is it important?**   10

3 **The life of teams**   26

4 **Team membership**   39

5 **Teamworking skills**   52

PART 2
Applying teamworking skills in practice   65

6 **Working in organisations**   67

7 **Multidisciplinary teams**   79

8 **Inter-professional collaboration**   91

9 **Teamwork as a student**   102

10 **Conclusion**   112

    References   120
    Index   124

Acknowledgements

Single authors cannot claim to work autonomously. In writing a book about teamwork I have been conscious of influences and help amounting to a supportive team around me. I would like to thank the Open University Press and McGraw-Hill Education editorial and production teams, particularly commissioning editor Katherine Hartle for her enthusiasm and encouragement.

Those that have influenced me include social work practitioners, university students, service users and carers; also work colleagues, particularly the social work staff team at the University of Kent. Practitioner colleagues allowed me to quiz them about their experiences of working in and managing teams. They include Margaret Eniola, Keith Gulvin, Sara Taylor, and several members of the Redvers Children's Referral Assessment and Support Team in Medway. I am most grateful to them all.

My wife, Kay affords me boundless support and, not being a social worker, naïvely questions my assumptions in a challenging and helpful way. We make a good team.

PART 1
Overview of teamworking

1 Introduction

When I told my wife that I would be writing a textbook on teamworking skills, she was supportive as always but expressed some puzzlement and wondered whether I would find enough to say about working in teams to warrant a whole book. As you start to read this introduction you may have similar reservations. Isn't teamworking as simple as a group of people engaging in 'combined action', as the *Oxford Dictionary* (2012) suggests? Why a textbook about it? The dictionary definition adds that teamwork is the combined action of a group, 'especially when effective and efficient', so immediately effectiveness and efficiency are outcomes that invite exploration. When considering teamworking skills for social workers, we may also question what we mean by a 'team', taking into account factors such as its constitution, setting, size and membership, and what skills are necessary to work as a team.

One other obvious and fundamental aspect is worth highlighting – a team is a group of human beings. When humans are involved in combined action, interacting and working together, the complexity of interpersonal relationships could potentially take several volumes to explore and analyse. You will be able to judge the need for and usefulness of a textbook on teamworking skills for social workers when you reach the Conclusion. To set the scene, later in this introduction there is a review of the chapters that follow and some suggestions for ways of interacting with the book.

As human beings we are social animals. Our first experience of interacting with others is family life, and from infancy and childhood, through play, school and other social activities, we learn to relate to others. Families vary in size, cohesiveness, acceptable behaviour and resources. Family cultures can include the involvement and influence of extended family members. Education normally takes place within a group and is a social activity. When we start work we depend on and relate to others. And this is the case when you train for and become a qualified social worker. Teamwork involves working with others, so it would seem to be a natural activity.

However, we all differ as individuals. When tackling a work task, some of us prefer to discuss it with others, plan together and consult colleagues, while others feel more comfortable reflecting and coming to conclusions alone.

Reflection

What are you like as a social worker when a service user is allocated to you? Do you immediately want to discuss the information and think through possibilities with others; or do you prefer to read through, make notes and reflect alone?

After an interview with a service user or a home visit do you want to talk about it with colleagues as soon as possible; or think through implications on your own?

Teamworking

This textbook starts from the premise that teamworking is not necessarily intuitive and that we all need to learn teamworking skills, or become more aware of and develop skills that we already have. The capability to work as part of a team does not emerge without purposeful effort, so we need to consider theoretical ideas that help us understand human relationships and collaborative working, develop appropriate skills and work to professional values that support teamworking. This book takes a broad view of what teamwork is, assuming it includes working towards agreed goals within our immediate work team and collaborating with other professionals when working towards a common purpose.

As we all have to relate to others in our work, it is more satisfactory and enjoyable to have good working relationships and cooperate with them. Maslow (1954) proposed a hierarchy of human needs that have to be met for us to develop towards self-actualisation. Once more basic needs are met, there are those relating to 'belonging' and 'esteem'. A sense of belonging can come from our experiences within families and friends but can be reinforced by the satisfaction of belonging to an effective work team. Self-esteem leading to confidence and achievement is dependent on having the esteem of others through their respect and recognition. Well-functioning teams provide this. Thus teamworking is a positive goal, potentially leading to more effective and efficient work. For social workers, this results in a better service for, and enhanced working with, people who use services and carers.

Teamwork also influences those aspects of your work that you usually undertake alone. Because teamwork offers opportunities to discuss your work and learn from colleagues within a particular team culture, the experience of teamworking will shape the way you think about and approach interviews with service users and home visits, making assessments, writing reports, planning, and generally undertaking and evaluating your work. A team will determine the resources you have at your disposal to help you. Social workers are normally part of teams and it is not possible to physically opt out. Arguably, you can withdraw emotionally but in so doing you will be a negative influence and make work life more difficult for both colleagues and yourself.

In writing about teamworking, I can draw on personal experience. I have some forty years' professional experience and have been a member of a number of teams and a team leader. Settings I have worked in include the Probation Service, the voluntary sector and higher education institutions. However, beyond my own experience, I can draw on that of others as well as on academic sources. I have learnt much from service users, colleagues and students.

Who is this book for?

This textbook is written for social workers at all levels but especially those who are at an early stage in their careers. If you are a qualified practitioner, the aim is that you will be able to relate the material covered in each chapter to your own experience. The book will also be of interest and help to you if you are a social work student as you prepare, eventually, to join a team as a qualified social worker. In addition, many aspects of teamworking, but particularly those outlined in Chapter 9, also apply to how students interact and work together during their degree programme and to becoming part of a team when undertaking practice placements. The book will also be applicable to practitioners in other professions, especially those in health and social care multidisciplinary teams. There are many types and sizes of teams but most teamworking principles are common to different settings and circumstances.

Book structure

The book is divided into two parts. Part 1 begins with an overview of teamworking, and its underpinning theoretical knowledge, skills and values. Following this introduction (Chapter 1), which acknowledges the variety of professional teams that involve social workers, Chapter 2 explores what teamwork is and its importance. It reviews characteristics of teams, definitions, size, the complexity of human relationships, and the potential for teams to be effective and efficient. It explores theoretical considerations that help understand teams and explain interactions between team members.

Chapter 3 focuses on the life of teams, considering stages of team development, dynamics, ethos and the culture of teams as holistic units. The chapter explores the positive outcomes that result when paying attention to three interconnected and overlapping aspects of teamworking – achieving a team's task, maintaining team cohesiveness and meeting the needs of individual team members. It proposes that a team as an entity amounts to more than the sum of its individual members. In contrast, Chapter 4 focuses on the characteristics of the individuals who are part of a team and the formal and informal roles they play, functional and team roles, including the role of leadership. Within this context, the chapter discusses relationships and conflicts that are part of team dynamics. It considers the implications of new members joining teams and established members leaving them. As it focuses on individual team members, this chapter also explores the importance of emotional intelligence and resilience, and the concepts of self-leadership and personal development.

Although the whole of the textbook addresses topics relating to skills needed for effective teamworking, Chapter 5 more specifically reviews particular skills and personal qualities necessary for social workers to participate successfully as team members.

Towards the end, the chapter includes a skills checklist outlining skills previously explored, inviting you to rate your capability for each of them and plan ways of developing those skills for which you score yourself low.

The remaining chapters constitute Part 2 of the book with the aim of applying teamworking skills to practice. Chapter 6 explores how being part of teams relates to working in organisations, since most organisations, particularly large bureaucratic ones, can be conceptualised as networks of teams. The chapter considers organisational and team culture and the implications for individual and team responsibility, accountability and liability. It includes examples of how teams are structured within organisations and highlights the importance of supervision, including group and team supervision.

Chapters 7 and 8 focus on social workers teamworking with other professionals. Chapter 7 considers teamworking applied to multidisciplinary teams that bring together a number of practitioners from different professional disciplines and are located in one work base. It outlines factors that help and hinder effective work in multidisciplinary teams and reviews the skills needed to work effectively in them. Taking the ideas from Chapter 7 further, Chapter 8 addresses the teamworking aspects of inter-agency collaboration and partnership – professionals from various agencies that collaborate and work in partnership to help a common service user but not necessarily as part of an identifiable permanent team in one location. It reviews the barriers and obstacles to collaboration and outlines the skills needed and actions that can be taken by professionals to overcome difficulties, qualities of a practitioner and underpinning social work values in inter-professional and multi-agency collaboration.

As mentioned above in relation to clarifying who this book is for, Chapter 9 considers collaborative working as part of a year cohort of social work students, in small informal and formal groupwork projects that are often part of learning and assessment, and in practice placements. The chapter draws on previous material covered in the book such as stages of team development, personal and cultural factors, team dynamics and tensions and relates them to the student experience.

Chapter 10 summarises the contents of the book, reinforcing some important learning points, reviewing characteristics of effective teams, and encouraging you to continue reading, pursue further sources of information and develop your skills.

Interacting with the book

As the chapters follow a logical sequence, it is often useful to have covered material from earlier chapters as you move on to later ones. However, as you take note of the content of individual chapters, you may want to read that chapter – or a section of it – first or for a specific purpose. Textbooks need not necessarily be read from cover to cover as one might a novel. You may have come across the idea that it is useful to 'gut a book'. Gutting a book involves looking through the list of chapters and the index to get a sense of what is included in it. Chapter subheadings are also a good guide to the book's contents. Read this introduction (Chapter 1) and the introductions to individual chapters as they briefly outline their content. All chapters also end with a chapter summary, so reading those enables you to review what the chapter covered. Chapter 10 provides an overall conclusion and summary. Having done all or some of this gutting, you can also skim read chapters.

In addition to the characteristics outlined above, the book has additional features that will help you interact with the material. It includes reflection points to encourage you to stop and think about yourself and issues related to the content that follows, thus applying these to your own experience. You will already have come across a reflection point above in this introduction. It is a good idea to write down your reflections for future reference. Other stopping points involve activities to help you consider and take further aspects of what is being presented. You can enter into reflection and complete activities individually or as a team, allowing a group of you to compare notes. Such team involvement enables you to interact with and discuss ideas put forward in the book but can in itself be seen as an opportunity for team building.

Another feature of the book is case examples to illustrate the implications of teamworking in practice. The aim of these examples is to highlight how teamworking can apply to the real world of work with its strengths and practice dilemmas. Discussion of these case examples as a team would also provide opportunities for team building and development. At the end of each chapter are suggestions for further reading. These will enable you to pursue topics further through more in-depth or related reading.

Limitations

Merely reading this book will not make you an effective team player or result in you automatically having excellent teamworking skills. Interacting with the book in the ways suggested above, including discussion within your team, will take you further than reading alone. In addition, you will need to accept challenges, develop your self-awareness and emotional intelligence, and try things out in your practice. Make suggestions within your team and aim to alter your behaviour as necessary and develop your skills.

This is an introductory text, so it has its limitations. Other books could be, and have been, written on relevant underpinning theories, and on practice situations such as working in organisations, multidisciplinary work, multi-agency and inter-professional collaboration. One aim of this book is to begin to enhance your awareness of teamworking issues, identify skills that you may need to develop, and encourage you to research ideas and read further. The book addresses teamworking in social work generically, and does not focus on any particular service user group or setting. It would be possible to write textbooks in more depth about specific areas of work such as social workers in children and families' teams collaborating with other professionals, community mental health teams or youth offending teams.

The focus of this book and its case examples, which include work with a variety of service user groups, is on community-based social work. Although many principles apply to other settings, this book does not specifically address residential or day care. Residential and day care are group settings and have staff teams but they have distinct characteristics, including, in residential care teams, having to cover shifts that span 24 hours a day and in both settings working intensively with service users, spending full days or 24 hour cover with them. The staff team experience involves interaction with service users in a way that social workers in community settings are not required to undertake.

This textbook is not about team leadership and group facilitation – that would require another volume. The book focuses on understanding teams and highlighting the skills needed for teamworking. There is a danger when a team is not effective to assume that the main or only reason for it must be poor team leadership. While a team leader can have a considerable influence on team development, culture and ethos, every team member has some responsibility for team effectiveness and efficiency. This book examines the role of leadership as one that can be shared by team members; it does not explore in depth the functional role and skills needed to be a team leader or manager.

Service user and carer participation

You will have noted above that work teams that include social workers in community settings do not normally have the intensity of daily interaction with service users that teams in residential and day care experience. That is not to say that the participation of service users and carers in the teams that this book explores should be overlooked. Part of effective teamwork involves having a clear purpose and achieving the team's aims and objectives. The primary purpose of social work and its aims and objectives must be to provide the best possible service to the people who use those services. Their involvement in assessing need, planning, commissioning and evaluating services is crucial and is in keeping with professional social work values.

Chapter 6 reviews a whole systems approach to develop service user and carer participation in organisations. It involves the organisation in developing a culture, structure, effective practice and effective review systems that include the participation of the people who use the organisation's services. Chapter 7 suggests that a service user can be considered a member of a multidisciplinary team, arguing that someone who has a diverse team of different professionals discussing their welfare should be entitled to the chance to contribute.

Throughout the book, I mainly use the term 'service users' when referring to people who use services and carers, being aware that there are other terms that individuals or organisations prefer, such as being an 'expert by experience'. Although I use other terms for contrast or specific emphasis, you should assume that by 'service user' I mean any user of the services of social workers, including carers.

Professional Capabilities Framework

It is interesting to be writing a book about skills needed by social workers at a time when the profession has adopted a Professional Capabilities Framework (PCF) (The College of Social Work, 2012) applicable to all practitioners, from pre-qualification students to newly qualified practitioners and onwards throughout their careers. The focus on a holistic capabilities framework is a shift from the previous more mechanistic emphasis on demonstrating competence through National Occupational Standards. However, both capability (the ability to accomplish something and potential to develop it further) and competence (a measure of having successfully accomplished something) involve learning, developing and using skills.

The PCF for social workers has nine domains or areas and although they are interdependent, detailed capabilities have been developed outlining how social workers are expected to evidence each area in practice at various levels of a student and social worker career. The domains that most closely relate to the development of teamworking skills are as follows:

> 1. Professionalism – Identify and behave as a professional social worker, committed to professional development.
> 2. Values and ethics – Apply social work ethical principles and values to guide professional practice.
> 5. Knowledge – Apply knowledge of social sciences, law and social work practice theory.
> 6. Critical reflection and analysis – Apply critical reflection and analysis to inform and provide the rationale for professional decision-making.
> 8. Contexts and organisations – Engage with, inform, and adapt to changing contexts that shape practice. Operate effectively within own organisational frameworks and contribute to the development of services and organisations. Operate effectively within multi-agency and inter-professional settings.
>
> (The College of Social Work, 2012)

In this introduction to the themes of the book and through the following chapters, you will be aware of specific and implied references to relevant PCF areas and their relation to teamworking skills.

2 What is teamwork and why is it important?

Introduction

This chapter will review the characteristics of teams, focusing on those that include social workers, considering definitions, size, the complexity of human interaction, and the potential for teams to be effective and efficient. It will explore theoretical considerations that help understand teams and explain the interpersonal relationships and transactions between team members.

Social workers are rarely autonomous professionals working completely independently. When you become a newly qualified social worker and as you change jobs throughout your career, you join a team. Owing to the nature of their role, social workers need to work in collaboration with colleagues and other professionals, thus engaging in various forms of teamwork. Teams vary in size, style, cohesiveness, communication, culture and in many other ways, and throughout this book we will explore such variables and their influence on teamworking.

Defining a team

There is no one definition of what a team is and the term can apply to a close knit group of individuals working in the same room or building and to open networks of professionals from different disciplines and organisations.

Definitions of a work team, in various textbooks and when searching the internet, usually include certain elements, such as a team being a group of people who:

- are interdependent;
- have complementary skills and roles;
- work collaboratively towards a common purpose, aims and objectives;
- ultimately achieve agreed tasks or results.

In addition to these characteristics that tend to be included in some form in most textbook definitions of a team, Bayliss (2009) – writing specifically about teams in health care – adds two thought-provoking ones:

- 'The members are identifiable by the name of the team to which they belong.' (Bayliss, 2009: 4)
- 'The team should be capable of working as a single unit. It is this characteristic which can reveal the strengths and weaknesses of a team and is where the dynamics are most evident.' (Bayliss, 2009: 6)

So, although they have some of the above characteristics, a collection of people standing together for the common purpose of waiting for a bus, or a number of students inter-acting as they discuss an academic topic in a group seminar, are not a team. Arguably, a senior departmental management group or a committee in a local authority need not be a team either. The director of a local authority department or chairperson of a committee may have no need to work collaboratively with other officers and members and those groups may not be interdependent.

The team characteristics outlined thus far support the idea that 'Teams can provide unique opportunities, they can make things happen which would not happen if the team did not exist' (Woodcock, 1989: 4). In a timeless textbook from a veteran manage-ment author, Adair (1986: 140) points out: 'Although there are tasks that do not strictly demand team work it does make a difference if they are tackled by a team. In other words, if there is a team it will approach these tasks in a different way from a mere collection of individuals.'

Team size

You may wonder how many people constitute a team, so let us consider minimum and maximum numbers. You will probably agree that a team has to be more than one person! There are certain jobs such as 'trucking' (you can search for this on the internet) for which job agencies advertise for 'husband and wife team' drivers. There have been some famous comedy duos and television presenters such as Ant and Dec, who won the British National Television Awards 'Best Entertainment Presenter' for ten years in a row. Reviewers say they make a 'good team'. These examples suggest that as few as two people can be referred to as a team. Or perhaps two persons might work as 'a team', or sub-team, within a larger team of people. This would make sense if the two people concerned are interdependent, have complementary skills and roles, and work collab-oratively to achieve a task and good results, thus displaying characteristics included in definitions of teams as previously outlined.

How large might a group of people be and still constitute a team? In sport, basket-ball has five team members playing at any one time, netball seven, football eleven and rugby thirteen, although the number of individuals in these 'teams' allows for a larger pool of players to choose from. Comparing work groups to sport teams can be a helpful analogy that we will return to in this book. You might at this stage consider how various sport teams relate to the characteristics included in the definitions of a team. The optimum size of work teams has been debated over the years, with writers point-ing out that if a team is too large it will be more difficult for team members to be interdependent and work collaboratively. Skills and roles may be unnecessarily duplicated. It is worth noting that as far back as the nineteenth century Maximilian

Ringelmann, a French agricultural engineer born in 1861, discovered that the more people who pulled on a rope, the less effort each individual contributed. That interesting early observation probably has implications for the optimum size of work teams.

The social work teams that we will be considering in this book may be quite small (single figures) but often consist of 20–30 people, this being the likely size of a group that you would join within an organisation. An interdisciplinary or multi-agency group of people that might be involved with a service user is likely to vary from two or three professionals to as many as twelve or more. Many of the issues discussed and skills outlined in this book will apply also to larger work and student groups, but you must remember that as numbers increase it becomes more difficult to show the characteristics of the elements that define a team.

As we shall see in exploring teamworking, communication and relationships are of great importance. There is a formula to work out the number of possible interactions in any group:

$$\frac{N \times N - 1,}{2}$$

where N is the number of members in the team. Thus in a team of 15 people, there are $15 \times 14 (15 - 1) = 210 \div 2 = 105$ possible relationships that influence communication, interdependence and collaboration. This is a reminder of the complexity of teams that consist of diverse individuals, both personally and professionally. It is important therefore to understand teams and have the skills to participate in them.

As already mentioned, teams may work in one room or building. The majority of local authority social services departments have open plan offices, sometimes large enough to accommodate two or three teams, where team members can readily interact formally and informally but where it can also be difficult to concentrate on individual work. A 'team' may also be geographically scattered. A family needing help and support may be in contact with a social worker, health visitor, school staff, general practitioner, a professional from a Community Mental Health Team, a family or children's centre, and others. Although from different professional disciplines and work agencies, they should be working interdependently and collaboratively as a team on agreed goals and tasks for the benefit of the family. This is something we will discuss further in Chapter 7.

Synergy

Although teams consist of diverse individuals, they have group characteristics, dynamics, culture and a 'life' (which will be explored further in the next chapter) of their own. The term 'synergy' has been used to describe the concept that an effective team is more than the sum of its parts. The word comes from the Greek root *synergos*, meaning 'working together'. It is used in science – water, a compound of hydrogen and oxygen, is an example of two elements coming together to produce a result that cannot be obtained independently by the constituent elements. Similarly, synergy is the ability of a team to perform better than its best individual member.

The combined action of team members having a good range of relevant team-working skills will contribute to team effectiveness – its success in completing its tasks and achieving its purpose, aims and objectives; and team efficiency – the team being well organised, competent and having the optimum number of people to cope with its work effectively.

Because teams are made up of human beings, a number of variables will affect the relationships and interactions between people, which can have an effect on the ability of a team to complete tasks and achieve results. In the rest of this chapter, we will consider some theoretical ideas that can help us to understand how people interact.

Theoretical considerations

From psychology and social psychology we will draw on psychodynamic approaches, including comparisons with cognitive behavioural theories, and transactional analysis. We will also consider the relevance of ecological and systems theories in understanding the context and environment of teams at macro, meso and micro levels, recognising that teams do not exist in isolation but are affected by many outside factors.

Early psychodynamic theories were proposed by Sigmund Freud (1856–1939) and led to psychoanalytic models to explain behaviour as arising from inner motives developed in early childhood. Three theoretical constructs within this tradition, familiar in psychotherapy, can help us to understand how people relate to each other in teams:

- Unconscious processes that influence meaning
- Transference – how past relationships affect the present
- Defence mechanisms that we use as a barrier or self-protection

Unconscious processes

Although he was not the first to express the idea, Freud is regarded as having 'discovered' the unconscious mind. Inner dynamic conflict during our upbringing results in unconscious thought processes, repressed feelings, habits, 'Freudian slips' of the tongue, desires and perhaps even phobias. Psychodynamic theories can be criticised for delving into hidden aspects of the human psyche, the influence of which on our behaviour is difficult, if not impossible, to prove. However, cognitive psychology suggests behaviour can become automatised through repetition and this seems to support psychodynamic ideas.

It may help us when faced with an anxiety-provoking task, such as making a presentation to a team, to go into 'automatic pilot' to present in a well-rehearsed way. Conversely, we may have a negative inner 'cognitive script' that unconsciously makes us believe we are not competent to achieve the task and affects our performance. Control of our behaviour is thus governed by unconscious processes that may affect our social perception and social judgements. Studies of perception, learning and memory (Power, 1997) suggest unconscious processing operates in a rather stereotypical fashion. Chapter 7 discusses stereotyping further in relation to multidisciplinary teams.

Implications for social workers are that we may develop set unconscious patterns of behaviour as practitioners. We may resent anyone, including colleague team members, who challenge our way of thinking and behaving. We may infer irrational meaning to the motives of others who behave differently from us.

Transference

Have you ever found another person difficult to relate to without really knowing why or, alternatively, found yourself drawn or attracted to someone even though you may know very little about them? Psychodynamic theory suggests that this may happen because we are unconsciously transferring or redirecting feelings from someone significant to us, probably in our childhood, to another person. The phenomenon occurs in daily life, not just in therapy where a patient's transference of feelings on to the therapist and the therapist counter-transference of feelings towards the patient is explored therapeutically.

Research since the original theorising suggests transference might be understood as social cognition where mental representations of people significant to us – 'significant others' – can be activated and used in responding to new people that resemble the person that was significant to us. Andersen et al. (1995) conducted research in which someone described their father as 'interested in politics, athletic and not very happy'. Later research participants were presented with a description of another person as 'interested in politics' and 'athletic' among other qualities. When asked to recall this description, participants tended to add 'not very happy' to the list. Such research suggests that a new person can trigger a mental representation of a significant other, leading us to make inferences that are not based on factual information.

Emotionally charged material is also triggered in transference and it can produce shifts in our self-concept. Furthermore, we may elicit from another person the very kind of behaviour experienced with the significant other, thus creating a self-perpetuating cycle.

What are the implications of this for teamworking? We may transfer expectations from one person or professional to another. If my father or mother were strict, I might expect and anticipate my team leader to be strict. You may have known an authoritarian medical consultant, so you will expect another one in a multi-disciplinary team to be so as well and respond to that person accordingly. This could trigger certain emotions in you such as feeling inferior, like a 'child'. You may behave in a way that elicits an authoritarian response.

Case example

On completing her social work programme and gaining her qualification, Vania was successful in obtaining a newly qualified social worker post in a Community Mental Health Team (CMHT). She was pleased and excited, although somewhat anxious. Her final statutory placement had been in an elderly persons' care management team, so when she started at the CMHT she felt she still had a fair deal to learn about mental health, psychiatric diagnoses and medication, frequently mentioned within the team. Although she had been an able student and obtained a good class degree, she increasingly felt helpless and inferior in her new team. It seemed to her that the rest of the team members were far more knowledgeable, skilled and competent than her. Her body language mirrored her feelings. Although she was tall, she tended to bow her head or tilt it to one side, slump her shoulders and down turn her eyes. She found herself biting her nails as she used to do when she was a little girl. She thought others were expecting too much of her and felt she was not capable of meeting their expectations.

The team leader reminded her of a professor at the university she attended. When she started the course she was in awe of him and found it difficult to call him by his first name as he expected. Her Eastern European family background led her to regard a professor as someone of high status. When Vania spoke to her team leader, she found it difficult to maintain eye contact and she had to swallow and clear her throat as her mouth became dry. She was unsure as to how to relate to him and tended to be apologetic about what she perceived as her slowness to integrate into the team. In return, the team leader showed concern and gave her advice but more like a father than a fellow professional.

Defence mechanisms

Defence mechanisms are coping strategies we use when faced with the anxiety produced by unconscious inner conflicts. They involve some self-deceit and include *denial* of unpleasant or threatening experiences, *rationalisation* of motives we find painful, *projection* of unwanted thoughts and feelings onto external objects (including people close to us), and *displacement* of anxiety-provoking instinctual wishes onto more acceptable activities or people.

The clinical based theorising about defence mechanisms from a psychodynamic tradition seems to be supported by cognitive behavioural theories (Brewin and Andrews, 2000) that suggest mental activity such a rumination or distraction can be used to block retrieval of thoughts or mental images that we fear or find anxiety provoking. As social workers in our work setting we may:

- deny that we are facing any relationship problems within a team and fail to confront and address those issues;
- rationalise reasons for lack of collaboration and poor team cohesion, explaining or justifying shortcomings with 'logical', plausible reasons, even if they are not true, and ignoring the emotional impact on the team. Some rationalising may help us analyse issues facing the team, but too much makes us cold and distant and negatively affects interaction between team members;
- project problems and difficulties on to external factors (e.g. management; professionals in other agencies or in other teams within our agency) when it might be more productive to explore them within the team;
- displace uncomfortable negative feelings on to 'acceptable' targets (e.g. join in complaining about new or less experienced members of the team, take work frustrations home, and unfairly blame relatives and friends for how we are feeling or, ultimately, 'kick the cat' in anger).

Transactional analysis

The intricate psychodynamic theorising about human relationships was adapted and popularised by Eric Berne (Berne, 1973) by proposing that interpersonal transactions between people can be understood as 'games' that people play. Transactional analysis, or TA, suggests that our personalities consist of 'ego states' or frames of mind that develop through early upbringing and subsequent experiences. The three basic ego states, not dependent on a person's age, are the Parent (P) – the tendency within us to nurture and discipline others; the Adult (A) – our logical and objective outlook on life; and the Child (C) – involving infantile feelings such as insecurity or playfulness. These concepts are not unlike the superego, ego and id in psychodynamic theory. One way of analysing transactions between people is to visualise them as a person relating from one of their ego states to that of another person.

An Adult-to-Adult way of communicating is the ideal transaction in professional relationships where work colleagues engage in clear communication and are able to discuss issues honestly and openly, are able to disagree with each other but respect each other's professional judgements, and interact in ways that lead to positive working relationships (Figure 2.1).

A possible Parent–Child submissive relationship might be the result of team members interacting from their Parent ego state, which can be a sign of concern but is often critical. They may assume an 'expert' role due to seniority, experience and qualifications, age, gender, strong personality, cultural background, or a combination of some or all of these characteristics. In TA jargon, a controlling Parent 'hooks' a sometimes angry child response. When a team member submits in this way, they tend to act like the 'child' who needs advice, reassurance and permission from the 'parent' to make decisions or just to perform their role in the team. The team member relating from their

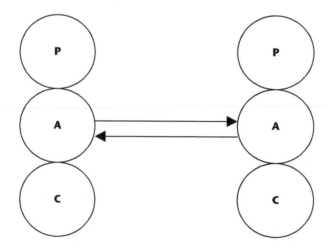

Figure 2.1

Child ego state to one or more colleagues in the team may be doing so due to being new, having less experience or qualifications, being younger, fitting into gender stereotypes, having a passive personality or behaving according to cultural traditions. This can create a dependent relationship and reinforce the 'parent' role of the other team member (Figure 2.2).

For a more sophisticated analysis, it is useful to note that both the Parent and Child ego states can be subdivided into two parts, one bringing together largely positive characteristics, the other mainly negative ones. These tendencies are summarised below.

- Nurturing Parent (NP) – caring, encouraging, sympathetic, concerned, protective, setting boundaries.
- Controlling (or Critical) Parent (CP) – judgemental, disparaging, demanding, condescending, patronising, angry, blaming.
- Free (or natural) Child (FC) – open, trusting, spontaneous, curious, playful, creative, intuitive, enthusiastic.
- Adapted Child (AC) – resentful, complaining, helpless, reluctant, apologetic, fearful, inferior, unsure.

CP–AC transactions (Figure 2.3) suggest a power relationship, where a team member may be literally overpowering towards colleagues, who consequentially find themselves disempowered. These dynamics can be the source of manipulation and friction within a team leading to some members becoming demoralised. A caring NP role can be helpful and is typically adopted by team members who are concerned about colleagues, supporting and helping them. FC behaviour can lighten the mood when team members laugh and joke together, 'let their hair down' occasionally and engage in fun social activities. However, as previously stated, Adult–Adult transactions are the ones that facilitate positive interaction and lead to the team's aims and objectives being achieved.

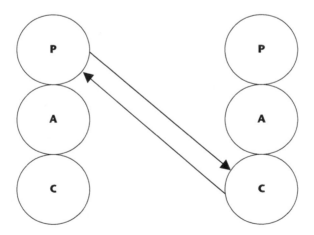

Figure 2.2

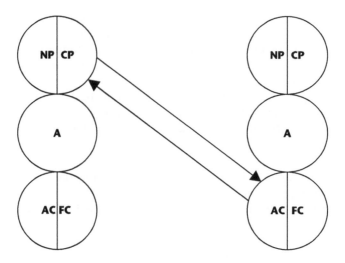

Figure 2.3

Reflection

Reflect on your team (or one you have recently been a member of).

- From which ego state do you mainly communicate and interact with other team members?
- Do you find yourself 'hooked' by the ego state of other team members? Do you have a tendency to hook them, or are your communications largely of the Adult–Adult kind?
- What TA transactions and behaviours (e.g. NP, CP, FC, AC) are you aware of in the team? Are these mainly positive or negative?

The 'drama triangle' (Karpman, 1968) encapsulates the dynamics in relationships that lead to interpersonal transaction 'games', which Berne (1973) initially outlined. Two team members can play the roles in rotation as they adopt shifting stances towards each other (Figure 2.4). The sequence may involve team member A being angry and irritated due to the perception that team member B is not 'pulling their weight' in support of the team. A becomes the 'persecutor', adopting a CP 'is all your fault' position and putting B in the role of 'victim'. B experiences AC 'poor me' feelings and may retort that there are personal and health reasons why they have not been able to commit themselves fully to the team. A might feel guilty to learn this and offer to take work off B, from an NP 'let me help you' position, thus becoming a 'rescuer'. B's angry response could be that A should not have jumped to conclusions and tells A this in no uncertain terms, thus themselves becoming the 'persecutor' treating A as the 'victim'. The 'game' can continue along similar lines as A and B change their positions round the drama triangle.

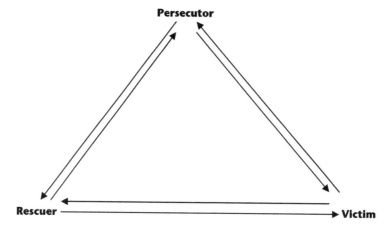

Figure 2.4

'Rescuer' team members typify the complexity of human emotions and inter-dependence, as they may be reluctant to rescue but experience guilt if they do not. They keep 'victims' dependent but often expect to fail in rescue attempts.

Ecological and systems theories

Systems thinking involves understanding what is happening within the context of a larger whole. To appreciate issues systemically literally means to put them into a context, to establish the nature of their relationships. If in our heavily industrial and chemical-dependent existence we release carbons and other substances into the atmosphere, it will damage the ozone layer. If we cut down and destroy rainforests, we will damage the whole ecological system. So we can borrow such concepts from nature to refer to a holistic approach to understanding interdependent human events and actions.

Systems theory can be traced back many years and initially included applications to engineering. A relatively modern example is to consider the central heating system of a building. If we experience extreme hot or cold temperature in the climate of one particular room, someone may have to investigate individual radiators, valves, thermostats, pipes that carry water around the system, or whether a central boiler in another part of the building is working to find the cause of the malfunction. Human systems are similarly interdependent and work together towards certain outcomes. A family is a system and so is a team. Interrelating parts consisting of individual team members and the interactions between them, as in family relationships, affect the overall functioning of the team and, conversely, the team's functioning and climate affects individuals and how they relate to each other.

Understanding teams as organic systems is another way of appreciating the complexity of human transactions and interactions. Since teams are human social systems, their reality can be socially constructed. Team practices are the construct, or common perceptions, of that particular team. Teams involve networks of conversation and communication in which accounts are created and more than one account of what is discussed can exist, none may be the truth, but all might be true – that is, meaning is context bound. The holistic context of teams involves wider macro, middle meso and closer micro levels.

Macro level

Teams are affected by many outside factors. Social work teams operate in a national political and social policy context. Governments develop policies and initiatives and generate legislation than can affect the role and function of social workers. It is important also to analyse political discourses, such as 'market society' trends leading to a 'mixed economy' of care and managerialism. Lymbery and Butler (2004) argued that 'partnership' in the late 1990s was a loose synonym for privatisation.

Macro-level developments that have influenced social work include: central government department changes in 2003 that saw responsibility for Children's Social Services transfer from the Department of Health to the then Department for Education and Skills; the Children Act 2004 establishing a duty for different agencies to cooperate; the development of a personalisation agenda summarised in the 2007 Government paper *Putting People First* that restructured ways of working with adult service users and community care; the setting up of a Social Work Taskforce in 2008 to review frontline social work practice and a Social Work Reform Board in 2010 to implement Taskforce recommendations. The Reform Board took account of the Review of Child Protection that the government asked Professor Eileen Munro to undertake, and of her final report in 2011. The Health and Social Care Act 2012 will result in professionals within adult services having to work closely with health professionals in a more integrated way. Work by the Reform Board has led to the introduction of a social work Professional Capabilities Framework (promoted by The College of Social Work launched in 2012) that will inform pre- and post-qualifying social work education and training from 2013. Many other such initiatives affect how social work teams work.

Meso level

Most social workers work within the context of large welfare bureaucracies and the macro developments mentioned above mean that as the landscape of social work and care management changes, organisational structures reconfigure and new cultures evolve. The central government department changes in responsibility led to meso restructuring of local authority departments with Children and Adult services becoming new and separate directorates or services.

For some years now, social workers have been part of interdisciplinary teams such as Youth Offending Teams and Community Mental Health Teams. Individuals are sometimes seconded into such teams, but the arrangements can involve being employed by a different organisation. Social workers can be located in schools, family centres, hospitals and health centres, as well as in more traditional local authority social services offices.

These meso implications highlight issues such as the location of social work, to whom social workers report and who might be a social worker's team colleagues. A social worker's team leader may not be a professional with a social work qualification.

Micro level

The macro introduction of a Professional Capabilities Framework and the meso trends in multi-agency and interdisciplinary work have implications at the micro team and individual level for the skills that social workers need and use through their career progression. The capabilities expected of a social worker at basic, experienced and advanced levels and in senior and supervisory posts influence the professional, functional and personal roles that practitioners assume within a team. The inspection and regulation of social work results in individuals having to account for their practice involving a good deal of paper (or computer) work.

Teams as systems

It can be helpful to have a systemic understanding of teams in terms of systems theory concepts. These may be familiar to social workers, as they can also be applied in practice such as family work to understand family dynamics. These are introduced briefly here but will be explored further in later chapters.

Like any system, teams will have *sub-systems* that may connect individuals together in ways that can be helpful and contribute to the team's work and accomplishments, or may be negative and create tensions and fragmentation. These sub-systems may be dependent on gender, ethnicity, friendships and allegiances. They may be the result of qualifications, knowledge, the individual's professional disciplines and previous experience. Status and formal and informal team leadership may also result in sub-systems.

Systems, and teams, have *boundaries*. These may vary in terms of how *permeable* they are. Very permeable teams will engage in considerable outward interaction with other teams and agencies. Payne (2000: 3) refers to this characteristic as 'open teamwork'. He suggests that 'the close relationships in the team are the basis for team members going outwards to the community, user or professional networks that they have contact with. As well as going outwards, they also draw these networks in to the team's work.'

However, permeability is a continuum and at the other end of permeable teams are those that are completely impermeable, closed and inward looking. Boundaries are defined by the communication that takes place across them and non-verbal communication, concerning emotional rather than cognitive issues, can influence external as well as internal interaction.

A team may have clear or somewhat more diffuse 'historical boundaries', not unlike inter-generational boundaries in families. These are the result of how the team has evolved over time; they are affected by reorganisations sometimes resulting in the merger of teams. An incoming newly appointed team leader will have boundaries to negotiate as they establish their role and leadership style. A team member being appointed team leader will also have boundaries to negotiate and historical issues relating to that individual's previous participation in the team's system will influence these.

Some sub-systems are hierarchically related. Leadership styles can range from dominant to a gentle influence, certain professionals assuming higher status in interdisciplinary teams and the perceived or sought status inherent in knowledge and qualifications can be factors in the development of hierarchies.

Permeable teams will be part of professional networks that can be conceptualised as *supra-systems* at the meso and macro levels. The network will involve other professionals and agencies outside the team but related to it. An eco map can be a way of exploring and representing these.

Understanding *circular* (rather than linear) *causality* provides insights into the dynamics within the life of a team and all aspects of how a team operates. The 'drama triangle' explored earlier is an example of a circular causality cycle (e.g. A causes B, B causes C, and C causes A) that can involve two or more individuals, rather than attributing outcomes linearly to one direct cause, which in interpersonal relationships can lead to blaming and scapegoating.

The social construction of reality mentioned above is highlighted by team *beliefs systems*. These provide a way of understanding and knowing the team's world and amount to an amalgam of team traditions, myths, legends, shared assumptions, expectations and prejudices. This will inform repeated patterns of thinking and behaving, or team *scripts* that suggest how a team typically responds to challenges and problems.

A team's stability and capacity for change can be understood through the concept of *homeostasis* or equilibrium. Theoretical ideas suggest that systems have a tendency towards stability. This would protect a team from chaos or disintegration. However, a capacity to change and adapt is equally important. This is the team's ability of organising itself in new ways more appropriate to changing circumstances. At any one time a team might be identifiable within a continuum from conforming, through flexible, to chaotic.

A *conforming* team will value conventionality over individual autonomy, will be intolerant of disagreement, rigid and closed to learning and change. A *flexible* team will allow room for individual autonomy, will be tolerant of disagreement, open to learning and to the development of new work patterns. A *chaotic* team will value individual autonomy over cooperation, will experience perpetual disagreement, ongoing crisis and constant change without learning.

Application to multidisciplinary and inter-agency practice

Granville and Langton (2002) outline a conference workshop where systemic and psychodynamic perspectives were discussed in the context of working across boundaries and negotiating relationships between different disciplines in therapeutic intervention with children and families. In commenting on some of the tensions encountered, they state: 'The potential for agencies and individuals to be seen as good or bad (with the related psychodynamic tendency towards *idealisation* and *denigration*), to be perceived a persecutory or abusive or negligent, is tremendously powerful' (Granville and Langton, 2002: 25, 26). They add:

> Professional workers are not immune from recourse to *denial as a defence* against the high levels of anxiety, anger, frustration, powerlessness and ambivalence generated towards service users, colleagues, managers and workers in other agencies in the course of often stressful, sometimes conflictual, from time to time confusing work situations. Thinking about our own experience when with a family, the transference and counter-transference within an overall systemic framework, our relationships and positions within the team, and how the wider network may be holding different aspects of the case, are all crucial parts of the work and provide important information.

Activity

Consider your current work team or a team that you have recently been part of. How does it measure up to some of the characteristics explored in this chapter?

(The activity can be undertaken by individual members of a team and then come together as a team to compare notes.)

My team has the following characteristics	Definitely not	Only to a limited extent	To some extent	Definitely yes	Evidence for your answer
Interdependent members who work collaboratively					
Achieves results					
Has a team name that identifies members					
Capable of working as a single unit					
Optimum size					
Synergy					
Open (not defensive) relationships					

(Continued)

Activity *Continued*

My team has the following characteristics	Definitely not	Only to a limited extent	To some extent	Definitely yes	Evidence for your answer
Adult–Adult transactions					
Aware of macro influences					
Positive meso landscape					
Effective micro functioning					
Permeable boundaries					
Positive belief systems					
Homeostasis (equilibrium, stability)					
Conforming					
Flexible					
Chaotic					

Chapter summary

This chapter has explored definitions of a team, pointing out that there is no one single definition but generally agreed characteristics such as team members being inter-dependent, having complementary skills and roles, working collaboratively towards common goals and being successful in achieving results. To these may be added an identifiable team name and the capacity to work as a unit. Within these characteristics, team size can vary from a few people to typical social work and multidisciplinary teams with 20–30 members.

The chapter has highlighted the complexity of interaction, relationships and communication in teams and the concept of 'synergy' – the potential for the effectiveness of the team to be greater than the sum of individual team members working alone.

Theoretical models to help understand human interaction were outlined, including: psychodynamic unconscious processes, transference and defence mechanisms; trans-actional analysis; and ecological and systemic approaches.

Further reading

There are no textbooks about teamworking in social work. General textbooks tend to concentrate on issues relating to teams in business settings and industry. Two textbooks that include discussion of group processes, interpersonal relationships and collaboration are:

Levi, D. (2007) *Group Dynamics for Teams*, 2nd edn. Thousand Oaks, CA: Sage.

Maginn, M. (2004) *Making Teams Work: 24 Lessons for Working Together Successfully*. New York: McGraw-Hill.

3   The life of teams

Introduction

Using different metaphors and models, this chapter will explore teams as a living and developing entity, progressing through typical phases. Some of the stages that teams experience involve tension and differences, which need to be managed. We will consider power issues and our responses to conflict. A discussion of needs related to achieving the team's task, developing and maintaining the team's cohesion, and fulfilling the aspirations of individual team members, will lead to some exploration of difficult work disputes and the possible need for mediation.

The concept of 'synergy' – the idea that an effective team is more than the sum of its individual members, discussed in the previous chapter – suggests that a team is a holistic unit and the complementary participation of its members gives it a character of its own. Reviewing definitions of teams in Chapter 2 we included the idea that a team should be capable of working as a single unit. Teams can have a mission statement, a purpose, aims and objectives, but they will also have an ethos, develop a culture and have a life identifiable through current characteristics and chronologically over the passage of time. Some teams are formed for a relatively limited period of time, such as a planning group for an event. Other work teams may be in existence for many years during which time new members join and established ones leave.

Developing teams

The metaphor of a living organism can be helpful in understanding the life of teams. It may not stretch the analogy too much to consider that a well-functioning team is a healthy team but that there may be times when a team might feel 'under the weather' or experience poor health, an ailment or disorder due to unstable dynamics as a result of internal tension or external pressures. A healthy lifestyle, balancing work on the task, maintaining team cohesion and meeting the needs of individual members, as we shall consider later in this chapter, are good aims.

Comparing the life cycle of a team to human growth and development we might envisage recognisable stages:

- *Infant.* Newly formed teams may be fragile and undeveloped, uncertain and insecure. They need nurturing to grow, through members getting to know each other and sharing issues.
- *Child.* Early in its life a team may have yet to establish an identity. It lacks maturity and needs to build resources and improve communication. Considering feedback will help members learn from mistakes and successes.
- *Adolescent.* There are times when teams will go through difficult transitions and may be rebellious and challenge authority within and without the team. A way through this will be to agree short-, medium- and long-term goals and plan for the future. An increase in self-knowledge and sharing strengths will help team members develop problem-solving skills and decision-making strategies.
- *Adult.* Mature teams are effective. Members communicate meaningfully with each other and interact well with an increase in active listening. There is a constructive use of conflict. Energy and commitment are hallmarks of a performing team. Values are agreed and there is the confidence to make links with other teams.
- *Older years.* A team that has developed over the years and adjusted to internal and external changes will have a good deal of collective knowledge and wisdom. There is a danger however that some teams stay together when their task is finished and become frail and ineffective. They avoid disbanding when acknowledging the end of their life would be the realistic thing to do.

Reflection

Focusing on your current work team (or teams that you have previously been a member of) consider the following questions:

1. Are you, or have you been, a member of an infant, child, adolescent, adult or older years team?
2. What team features and characteristics support your assessment of the stage the team is going through?
3. How can you contribute to help the team develop and grow?

In writing about groupwork, Benson (2010) outlines ideas that also apply to teams. Benson suggests that groups are organic and capable of evolving and puts forward group stages that focus on particular issues that include the need for parenting. Beginning stages contain inclusion issues such as nurturing. Middle stages address control issues, including power and autonomy. Later stages incorporate affection issues, which promote teamwork. The ending stage focuses on separation issues at physical, emotional and intellectual levels.

Models of group life

A number of theorists have suggested that small groups, including teams, tend to experience typical stages in a developmental sequence. One of the earliest was Tuckman (1965), whose model of group life has been quoted extensively and is still relevant. Tuckman suggested that a group progresses through five stages. Some groups will do so sequentially, although it is common for a team not to move through the stages 'neatly' and linearly but to skip a stage and regress or revert to an earlier one depending on circumstances. The stages relate to the life of a team over a period of time, but they may also be experienced to some extent each time a group comes together so can be applied, for instance, to a team meeting. The five stages are:

1. Forming. Interaction is typically anxious and uneasy. The team is uncertain about what behaviours are acceptable and has not yet established norms and procedures. Members will be testing each other out and this may be particularly so in an interdisciplinary team. Ways of working have not been agreed, so the mood is 'we seem at a loss' and 'I'm not sure how to proceed or where I fit in'. The appointment of a new team leader or manager has elements of a fresh start, and may result in a team reverting to a period of forming. In a team meeting, this stage may include awkward silences or procedural questions.

2. Storming. Interaction will include tension and conflict. There is emotional resistance to the task, perceiving it as too large or complex, so 'it can't be done' or 'I won't do it'. Team members may be jockeying for position and resent or blame each other. Splinter sub-groups may form. Emotions are more prominent than rational thinking. Threats, changes and reorganisations may trigger this behaviour in an apparently well-established team. In a team meeting, this stage will typically include disagreements and arguments that slow the flow of the agenda.

3. Norming. Norms emerge and ways of working are agreed. Earlier resistance diminishes as discussion and mutual support resolve conflicts. A sense of determination emerges with agreed suggestions for tackling the task and a feeling that 'we can do it' and 'I have a part to play'. When experienced team members leave and new ones join or when a team takes on new tasks, it may revisit this stage. In a team meeting, ground rules will be accepted and helpful suggestions for tacking issues are made and agreed.

4. Performing. Team interaction is purposeful with individuals collaborating to achieve the task. Members play complementary, helpful roles and interdependence replaces tensions. Individuals feel safe to express disagreements and openly discuss differences of opinion, finding acceptable compromises. The accomplishment of results leads to a feeling that 'we are doing it' and 'I am contributing to results'. In a team meeting, there will be energy, focus on the agenda, agreed action points and a feeling that the meeting is getting somewhere.

5. Ending. Teams that have come together for a limited period of time come to the end of their work. Individuals leave but there may be a sense of loss, not unlike bereavement, and a tendency to want to keep the team together even after the task has been completed. Endings can be positive with a sense of accomplishment, feeling 'we did it!' and 'I was part of it'. Alternatively, there can be negative endings when a team collapses or disintegrates and fails to achieve the task. A formal gathering to mark an ending can be meaningful. Suggestions to meet again for a reunion or further support are often made. In a team meeting, a good ending will be the result of having worked through the agenda and agreed the date of the next meeting. However, team meetings can end in a fragmented and unsatisfactory way with a sense of unfinished business. Naturally, this is frustrating for team members.

There are implications for team leaders in the above stages. Forming and norming are to be expected as stages to work through, so a leader need not feel personally responsible for uncertainty or tension. A leader can encourage team progress by facilitating norming and performing and working towards positive endings. The person who is chairing a team meeting has the responsibility to move through the agenda and point out if people are drifting from a point or taking too long over an item. However, team members should not expect that the leader will be solely responsible for a team progressing through its life stages. It is crucial that every team member is aware of the implications of stages and contributes towards forming a team, resolving disagreements and tensions experienced during storming, establishing team norms, actively performing and working towards positive endings.

Relational model

The psychotherapist Linda Schiller (Schiller, 2003) formulated a relational model of group development influenced by feminist thinkers, which she applied to women's groups. She went on to develop those ideas, applying them to mixed groups of vulnerable people experiencing trauma, oppression and loss. In stressing the importance of connection and affiliation for women, she was highlighting qualities that are relevant to any team but particularly those within the helping professions. I trust it is acceptable for a male writer to suggest that these stages provide insights beyond women's experience.

- *Pre-affiliation.* Members are getting to know each other and deciding whether the group is for them. The development of trust is important.
- *Establishing a relational base.* Bonds of affiliation and connection develop. Creating a sense of safety is important.
- *Mutuality and interpersonal empathy.* Intimacy develops and an empathetic understanding of each other is pursued, which helps members recognise their differences.
- *Challenge and change.* Having experienced connection and empathy, members feel free to challenge themselves, each other and facilitators. This allows growth to take place.

- *Separation and termination.* Endings are addressed and acknowledged.

There are some similarities with Tuckman's stages but Schiller's emphasis is more on developing relationships and self-awareness than on achieving tangible goals and tasks. The main goal in the relational model is arguably personal growth. A significant difference that may provide a helpful insight for social work teams is that in this model conflict and positioning emerges later, once members feel safe to challenge having established mutual connections and respect. It may be helpful to be aware of the difference between the 'storming' of an immature team and the 'challenge and change' that is possible in a mature team where members understand and respect each other.

Activity

Write down notes based on your experience, focusing on your current work team (or teams that you have previously been a member of).

1. Provide instances of having experienced teams (and team meetings) forming; storming; norming; performing; ending.
2. Provide instances of having experienced teams at the pre-affiliation stage; establishing a relational base; mutuality and interpersonal empathy; challenge and change; separation and termination.
3. Reflecting on these models, what features do you see as positive to help teams develop?
4. What features do you see as negative, blocking or slowing team progress?
5. From your experience, can you give examples of how the 'storming' of an immature team is different from the 'challenge and change' that is possible in a well-established team?
6. Is it inevitable that teams have to experience the whole range of stages? What evidence do you have to support your view?

Power issues

A team can be powerful and in an ideally performing team power will be equally shared so that each team member feels individually empowered to pursue the team's purpose, aims and objectives. However, teams are made up of diverse human beings, so it is almost inevitable that there will be actual or perceived unequal contributions. In a team meeting, some individuals naturally contribute verbally more than others. A strong or extravert personality may result in some team members being seen as more influential than others. Levels of ability will vary, so some individuals may be more capable than others at certain tasks. Some team members may be perceived, or see themselves, as having a higher status than others. There will be times when individual team members will feel that their voice is not being heard. They may experience feelings such as disillusionment, frustration and anger because their views are not accepted or they are not contributing as much as they feel they could.

The varying emotional needs of each team member and interdependent relationships lead to complex dynamics that can result in unhelpful sub-groups and isolated individuals. This storming can include tension, misunderstandings, strained relationships and unresolved issues. In meetings or general team interaction, people may use the work of the team as a vehicle to position themselves and address their own feelings and power dynamics. Team members may perceive a neutral comment about something they have done, not done or about the way they have done it as a personal attack on them. Individuals may be attempting to deal with their own emotional issues, so the meeting agenda or the team's task is slow moving or not accomplished.

It may be too much to ask that every team member's level of commitment and the extent to which they are 'signed up' to the purposes of the team should be uniform. Some conflict is inevitable and working openly towards a resolution can be creative. Although not painless, honestly discussing disagreements can result in better decisions being made. When dealing with difficulties, it is helpful for team members to be aware of their personal style or their orientation towards conflict.

Kenneth Thomas and Ralph Kilmann (Thomas, 2002) have identified five styles of responding to conflict:

- *Competing*. Competitive individuals focus on their personal goals. They see conflict as a win/lose situation and attempt to win at the expense of others. Their emphasis on the team's task is much higher than on relationships.
- *Accommodating*. Accommodating individuals yield or concede their opinions. They aim to appease others and tend to lose against competing team members. Their emphasis on the team's task is much lower than on relationships.
- *Avoiding*. Individuals with an avoidance orientation to conflict are reluctant or refuse to become involved. They tend to ignore conflict or keep it from surfacing by withdrawing. Their emphasis on the team's task is lower than on relationships.
- *Compromising*. The compromise style focuses on give-and-take. It involves negotiation and trade-offs. Individuals can be firm or flexible and their style results in some winning and some losing. Their emphasis on the team's task is higher than on relationships.
- *Collaborating*. Collaborative individuals focus on win/win solutions that involve discussion and understanding. This takes time. Their emphasis is as high on the team's task as it is on relationships.

No orientation to conflict style is necessarily right or wrong. Different kinds of conflict situations have differing requirements. In some circumstances, we may be very committed to our personal position and in others we may place a high value on harmony. There may be situations in which other team members may be very committed to their positions. If we always adopt the same orientation to conflict, there may be times when our behaviour is not appropriate to the situation.

Activity

Reflecting on your experience as a member of a team, or teams, answer the questions below:

1. On reading through the orientation to conflict styles above, was there one that you instinctively felt 'this is me'? If so, which one?
2. How does your 'natural' or preferred style help you manage conflict?
3. Can you recall situations when you have used other styles successfully? Which ones?
4. What led to your style being appropriate in such situations?
5. Are there one or more styles that you need to develop? If so, how might you tackle this?

Lessons that we all need to learn include being able to take a strong stand on matters involving important personal and professional principles; being willing to accommodate the views of other team members without perceiving them as a personal attack on us; being disposed to let go matters that are not as important to us as they may be to others; being able to negotiate compromises; and being prepared to devote enough time to collaboration with other team members.

Case example

A local authority instituted a single central telephone contact Service Users' Access Point, thus taking that function away from individual teams and established a borough wide Duty, Intake and Assessment Team (DIAT) to undertake initial assessments, previously carried out in geographical teams, and refer work on if appropriate to child protection and family support teams.

The reorganisation led to a child protection team losing some members to the newly formed DIAT and becoming a smaller and more specialised team. This produced uncertainty and insecurity, as the team had not yet established a new identity but were required to undertake work involving considerable risk. Their perception was that if serious cases were not managed effectively, it could result in individual social workers being blamed. A number of team members tended to put senior management in the role of 'persecutor' and saw themselves or the team as 'victims'. They looked to the team leader to be their 'rescuer'. A few 'competitive' individuals raised personal issues about their conditions of service with the team leader, threatening to 'work to rule'. The team leader felt that she was telling off naughty teenagers in dealing with these issues.

The acceptance of the situation by some 'accommodating' team members and the silence of 'avoiding' individuals, who ignored tensions and did not voice their opinion, tended to annoy 'compromising' team members who looked for negotiated solutions. Sub-groups and factions emerged, which produced storming in meetings. The team leader nevertheless brought as many of the issues as possible (other than personal ones) for discussion at team meetings and sought the support of 'collaborating' colleagues and to develop a 'collaborating' approach in others to help the team grow. One team member suggested a short start-of-the-week forum every Monday morning for information sharing and updates. This was accepted by the majority, became the norm and proved to be a helpful contribution towards the team tackling conflict in a constructive and mature way.

Three sets of needs – Task, Team, Individual

The influential management writer and leadership trainer John Adair proposed a model (Adair, 1973) that has been widely used, quoted and applied to teams, suggesting that a work group with a common aim or task has three sets of needs that must be met if they are to be successful (Figure 3.1).

The needs related to achieving the *task* include having:

- A clear purpose and task for the team.
- Agreed aims and objectives.
- Clarity about the individual responsibilities of team members.
- A plan to work towards agreed objectives setting out realistic targets and priorities.
- Support and resources such as appropriate working conditions, training and supervision.

The above points suggest every member of a team needs to agree what the team's purpose and task is and how to work towards it. It is quite common when a team takes time to discuss these issues for different viewpoints and emphases to emerge. The purpose can shift, such as in the case example above, due to reorganisations and changes of team name to reflect new policies and approaches. A helpful activity that a team can benefit from is to work together on a mission statement over a period of time. The

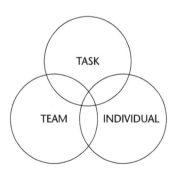

Figure 3.1

exchange of ideas and attempts to agree a succinct form of words that captures the team's priorities can be more significant than the actual statement that emerges, which inevitably will not be faultless.

The needs related to building and maintaining the *team* include:

- Opportunities for building teamwork and collaboration into individual job responsibilities.
- Genuine consultation, information sharing and good communication.
- Regular discussion of the team's aims and objectives.
- Regular team meetings.
- Agreed informal gatherings and social events.
- Acceptable team norms.
- Ways of enabling the team to progress through its life stages towards performing effectively.
- Strong team morale and cohesion.
- Support and resources such as an appropriate team size, mix of complementary skills and roles, and access to management decision-making.

This area highlights the need to meet regularly, formally and informally. Different meetings can be held as appropriate and include business, brief weekly updates, information giving and the gathering of team views for responses to management initiatives, reflection, case discussions, training and, as mentioned above, exploration of the team's purpose, task, aims and objectives. Regular and formal team meetings are necessary for sharing information, consultation and good communication. It is important for agreed action points to be recorded and checked at subsequent meetings. The frequency and variety of meetings will depend on the type of team and its workload at any one time. Although in a busy team there may be the perception that there is no time for formal meetings, the need for them is probably of greater importance at such times to monitor workloads and the achievement of tasks.

Informal team 'maintenance' activities are also significant. Coffee breaks and eating together as part of an appropriate team routine can provide excellent opportunities to build cohesion, catch up with the circumstances of individual team members, and informally discuss work issues of relevance to the team's purpose and current tasks. Other social gatherings can include agreed ways of acknowledging birthdays, someone leaving, Christmas and other religious and secular festivals. It is important that team members are involved in suggesting and organising events, and that no pressure is put on those that may not wish to take part due to specific reasons such as personal circumstances or religious views.

The needs of *individual* team members include:

- Being clear about their role, responsibilities and expected contribution to the team.
- Recognition of successful work undertaken and being given constructive feedback.

- Knowing their level of authority and how they fit into team interdependence.
- Regular supervision.
- Personal satisfaction and a sense of fulfilment.
- Support and resources such as induction for new team members, regular appraisal, training and fair employment conditions and facilities.

Some of these needs are met by organisational procedures and are the responsibility of a team manager or leader and senior practitioners. However, it is the responsibility of all team members to contribute to the above areas through developing positive relationships, cooperation, collaboration, mutual help, respect, acceptance and unconditional positive regard, qualities that will be revisited in Chapter 5.

Figure 3.1, with its three equal and overlapping circles, is a reminder that no one set of needs is more important than the others and that they overlap with one another rather than existing in isolation. It might be interesting to consider the implications of situations that distort the diagram with at least one of the circles being disproportionately larger than the others.

A large 'task' circle might suggest a team where undue emphasis is placed on achieving the task and the measurement of results to the neglect of building the team and meeting individual needs. A possible scenario could be the imposing of targets and priorities resulting in a team with low morale and unhappy and frustrated individual members.

A large 'team maintenance' circle might suggest too many meetings with lengthy discussion or team building training events that feel like the 'navel-gazing' of a self-absorbed team. These can leave individuals drained and possibly frustrated from inward-looking considerations that do not contribute to reaching aims and accomplishing the task. A related scenario might be a team that overdoes the holding of social gatherings and events. Members may have long meal breaks, enjoy each other's company and have a great social life but little work gets done.

A large 'individual needs' circle might suggests that addressing the needs of one or more individual team members is taking a disproportionate amount of time, to the detriment of achieving the task and team morale. It is not uncommon to come across individuals who are not the best 'team players'.

There is a probably apocryphal story that a team-building trainer emphasising the need for collaboration at work quoted the old saying 'There is no I in team'. A somewhat frustrated individual retorted, 'no, but there is an M and an E'. The annoyed trainer quickly came back with the response, 'well, yeah, but there is no U either, so shut up!'

Joking apart, there may be some individuals that may fear losing individuality if too much emphasis is placed on achieving a team ethos and no decision, whatever its nature, is made without full team discussion. It is salutary to note that a team that works well together can accept that emergency decisions might be taken by the team leader at short notice, that sub-groups might be delegated the authority to make plans that fit in with the overall purpose of the team, and that individual team members can be allowed creative and at times unorthodox contributions to team work or their expertise being used in specialist areas of knowledge.

Work disputes

Issues considered thus far in this chapter suggest that some inequality in the contributions, influence and capabilities of team members, their levels of commitment and the occasional conflict experienced within a team is inevitable. However, beyond these experiences the behaviour of one or more individuals may be very difficult for a team to deal with at times. Morrison (2007) explores the relevance of emotional intelligence to social work, a subject that is discussed further in the next chapter. Reflecting on the rationale and stimulus for putting forward his ideas, Morrison (2007: 247) states:

> as a mentor for managers and supervisors dealing with difficult staff management situations, it is increasingly apparent [clear] that the most troubling and intractable situations exist when performance difficulties occur in the context of staff who lack accurate empathy, self-awareness and self-management skills. This lack of emotional competence renders the specific performance problems, such as poor recording practice, all but unmanageable. In the worst cases, these become almost 'toxic' in such a way that whole teams or even agencies can become enmeshed in the distorting dynamics surrounding the individual staff member.

Team members that constantly challenge colleagues, have strong views, personal agendas and are over-competitive can create uncomfortable tension and be perceived at best as overpowering and ultimately as intimidating and bullying, leading to an unacceptable imbalance of power. Differences of opinion can result in personality clashes leading to entrenched relationship tensions between two or more individuals where it appears that a resolution is impossible. The emotional dimension of disagreements overtakes the objective consideration of issues and can result in the breakdown of work relationships. Unresolved conflict affects team cohesion and morale, results in time and energy being directed towards the disputes rather than the team's purpose and aims, and leaves individuals distressed and possibly experiencing physical and mental health problems that result in taking time off.

Disputes often take place within the established ways of working of the team and the rules and policies of the organisation. The behaviour of individuals is not necessarily illegal or against the agency's regulations, thus it is difficult to discipline those concerned and it leaves colleagues angry and frustrated when they expect team leaders and line managers to sort out difficult individuals.

Hard as such situations are, it is worth attempting to discuss them frankly as a team. This has to be handled very sensitively and there may be times when external help is advisable. Some organisations have a mediation service available as part of their Human Resources support or are willing to pay for it to be provided by external facilitators. However the process is organised, it should be voluntary and the mediators independent. With a neutral and impartial approach, mediators enable the exploration of issues and collaborative working towards agreements and resolution without apportioning blame. An ultimate and regrettable outcome can be an individual deciding that their position is untenable and choosing to leave the team.

Some form of independent mediation tends to be used as a last resort, although it is advisable not to leave it until relationships appear to have broken down irretrievably and conflicts become a formal matter. Mediation skills are useful for any team member to manage the ongoing disagreements and conflict that are an inescapable feature of team life. They include active listening, thinking innovatively, not being set in previous patterns of responding, finding common ground, creative responses and assertiveness. These will be discussed further in Chapter 5.

Chapter summary

This chapter has focused on the whole team as an entity or unit with a life of its own. The metaphor of the team as a living organism led to consideration of teams as an infant, child, adolescent, adult and as in one's older years. The chapter briefly outlined ideas about organic and evolving teams proposed by Benson (2010), the well-known model of group (or team) stages suggested by Tuckman (1965), and the relational model proposed by Schiller (2003) from a feminist viewpoint.

An interesting comparison between the latter two models was that whereas Tuckman suggests a 'storming' period before 'norming' and 'performing', Schiller proposes that 'challenge and change' is only possible after 'establishing a relational base' and achieving 'mutuality and interpersonal empathy'. It was suggested that this may be the difference between the 'storming' of an immature team and the 'challenge and change' that is possible in a well-established team.

We explored power issues and five personal styles or orientations towards conflict: competing, accommodating, avoiding, compromising and collaborating. Rather than intrinsically right or wrong, these were considered alternative approaches to meeting the requirements of different kinds of conflict situations.

The chapter included discussion of three sets of needs related to achieving the team's task, developing and maintaining the team's cohesion, and fulfilling the aspirations of individual team members, depicted as three equal and overlapping circles pointing to their equal importance and interrelatedness. Possible imbalance in the three areas was explored with scenarios highlighting the dangers of paying a disproportionate amount of attention to the team's task, to team building exercises or social gatherings and to the needs of one or more individuals. Serious work disputes between two or more individual team members were then considered with the possibility of ultimately seeking independent mediation. It was acknowledged that mediation skills are useful for all team members.

Further reading

Deutsch, M., Coleman, P. and Marcus, E. (eds.) (2006) *The Handbook of Conflict Resolution: Theory and Practice*. San Francisco, CA: Wiley. Although wide ranging and including aggression and violence, international, faith and religious, and family conflict, much of this textbook is applicable to interpersonal relationships and teams.

Lencioni, P. (2005) *Overcoming the Five Dysfunctions of a Team: A Field Guide for Leaders, Managers and Facilitators*. San Francisco, CA: Jossey-Bass. The five dysfunctions are: absence of trust; fear of conflict; lack of commitment; avoidance of accountability; inattention to results.

4   Team membership

Introduction

This chapter will focus on the characteristics of individuals who are part of a team. We will consider the contributions that team members make and the roles they play both formally and informally. In exploring the influence of different roles, we will see that contributions to the team can be positive and involve team members' strengths, but can also include inevitable weaknesses. We will consider the role of leadership, as a given function and as contributed by all team members, and briefly explore leadership styles, actions and skills. Exploration of team membership will lead us to revisit relationships and conflicts, also discussed in the previous chapter.

Within the context of team membership, we will also explore some implications of new members joining a team and who should be regarded as a member of the team (i.e. team boundaries). The focus of this chapter will also lead to discussion of individual emotional intelligence and resilience, broadening this to consideration of team resilience. The concept of self-leadership and personal development will also be examined.

Activity

Think of your experience within your current work team. Alternatively, you may recall a time when you were part of a previous work team or a small student study group. Consider the questions below. You may find it helpful to summarise your thoughts in writing.

* What responsibilities does each team member typically have?
* How are responsibilities shared among group members?
* What do you find helpful in the way individual team members contribute and participate?
* What is not helpful to team functioning?
* What is the style of the team leader?
* Do other team members play a leadership role?
* If so, is this helpful or not?

Characteristics of team members

In the above activity you may have thought of formal functions, such as a senior practitioner supervising other members of the team or someone agreeing to take the minutes of a team meeting. You may have considered contributions that seem to depend on the type of person each individual is – the one who more likely than not will have at their fingertips information required by other team members; the social person who enquires about others' wellbeing or brings in snacks to share; the critical, hard-to-please individual who seems to regularly find fault with other people and situations; the demanding or inflexible team member whose expectations can create tensions. There are those who always seem willing to readily take on work and some who appear to keep their head down and hope they will be overlooked when a new piece of work has to be allocated.

Leadership may lean towards the autocratic allocation of tasks and responsibilities, or towards a more cooperative and democratic style of decision-making. You may agree that caring, helpful team members, those who are good at planning or those who regularly enquire whether tasks have been accomplished are contributing a leadership role to the team without necessarily being the designated team leader.

Such considerations remind us that individuals play varying and different roles in teams and that the accomplishments of an effective team will be the result of the synergy to which all team members ideally contribute. Team roles have been researched and written about by a number of theorists. Typical roles encountered in most teams include those played by team members who are perceived by others as, for instance, a leader, a carer, a thinker, a doer or an achiever.

The work of Belbin (1991, 2010) based on years of research into management teams provides one of the most well known theoretical outlines in this area. Belbin (1991:161), who has developed Team Role theory, explains that the term 'team role' 'describes a pattern of behaviour characteristic of the way one team member interacts with another' and this tendency to behave, contribute and interrelate with others in a particular way 'serves to facilitate the progress of the team as a whole'.

Team roles and functional roles

Team roles differ from functional ones. *Functional roles* refer to the function that the team member carries out as outlined in their job description and dependent on their post in the organisational structure and specialist skills. Functional roles might include being a social worker, other professional and work titles, a secretary, administrator, team leader or manager. As outlined above, *team roles* describe personal behaviour, which will be influenced by an individual's personality and character. We have already mentioned possible team roles such as the creative person, the supporter of others, the questioner, the intellectual individual and the person who plays a leadership role. You will note that, interestingly, it is possible for 'leadership' to be a functional and a team role. The implication is that leadership is a task and purpose that belongs to the team. It can and should be helpfully shared by several, if not all, members of the team.

The type of contribution that an individual makes to the team will be dependent on their team role or roles. Belbin interestingly suggests that a positive and helpful team contribution may have a down side, but he refers to this other side of the performance coin as an 'allowable weakness'. There may be some reassurance for each one of us in accepting that we make varying beneficial but by no means perfect contributions to teams and that we are allowed our human flaws and limitations.

In practical studies centring on the composition of teams at the Administrative Staff College, carried out by the Industrial Training Research Unit, Cambridge, Belbin (1991) observed qualities helpful to achieving group results. The research was innovative in moving away from a focus on the behaviour of individual managers to that of management teams. It found that whereas no individual can combine all the qualities needed for effective work, a team of individuals can and often does. Team Role theory has subsequently been applied to a variety of work teams.

Belbin's research highlighted nine team role types outlined in Table 4.1. There have been other team roles classifications, some with fewer types, but Belbin's remains pre-eminent and is referred to in many textbooks.

Table 4.1 Belbin's team roles and their characteristics

Team role	Contributions	Allowable weaknesses
PLANT	Creative, imaginative, unorthodox Solves difficult problems	Ignores incidentals Too preoccupied to communicate effectively
MONITOR EVALUATOR	Sober, strategic and discerning Sees all options Makes accurate judgements	Lacks drive and ability to inspire others
COORDINATOR	Mature, confident, good chairperson Clarifies goals, promotes decision-making, delegates well	Can be seen as manipulative Offloads personal work
RESOURCE INVESTIGATOR	Extravert, enthusiastic, good communicator Explores opportunities Develops contacts	Over-optimistic Loses interest once initial enthusiasm has passed
IMPLEMENTER	Disciplined, reliable, conservative and efficient Turns ideas into practical solutions	Somewhat inflexible Slow to respond to new possibilities
COMPLETER FINISHER	Painstaking, conscientious, anxious Searches out errors and omissions Delivers on time	Inclined to worry unduly Reluctant to delegate
TEAMWORKER	Cooperative, mild, perceptive and diplomatic Listens, builds, averts friction	Indecisive in crunch situations

(Continued)

Table 4.1 *Continued*

Team role	Contributions	Allowable weaknesses
SHAPER	Challenging, dynamic, thrives on pressure Has the drive and courage to overcome obstacles	Prone to provocation Offends people's feelings
SPECIALIST	Single-minded, self-starting, dedicated Provides knowledge and skills in particular areas	Contributes only on a narrow front Dwells on technicalities

Reflection

Reflect on the nine team roles in Table 4.1.

- Do you recognise yourself in one or more of them? Which ones?
- Have you come across these roles in individuals within teams of which you have been a part?
- How do your reflections now compare with the notes you made as a result of the activity at the start of this chapter?

It may be that you see yourself and others in more than one of the roles. It is common to have two or three preferred roles or types that come naturally to us, and this will be so for other people as well. There are advantages in being able to play several team roles. A team with as few as four to six people, for instance, may account for all nine roles. Having the contributions of all the role types will provide balance and result in an increased likelihood that the team will be effective and accomplish its tasks.

When new appointments are made to a team, it is usual for the person specification and the selection process to focus on previous experience, skills and knowledge required rather than the candidates' behaviour, how they might personally contribute and inter-relate with others. However, it is possible to some extent to test the latter through interviews and other selection procedures, and teams that take this into consideration benefit from the balance of roles they achieve. When too many team members exhibit particular roles, the 'allowable' weaknesses can be over-emphasised to the detriment of effective team functioning.

Team roles will be influenced by gender, ethnicity, nationality, culture, education, self-awareness and self-knowledge. There is a danger of unconsciously or unthinkingly falling into stereotypes such as the expectation that a female team member will more likely be caring, sensitive and gentle and a male team member probably self-confident, objective and strong. Nonetheless, a gender and ethnicity balance in addition to a team role mix will benefit a team.

African-centred values (Graham, 2002) include strong kinship bonds and a tradition of communal self-help. These contrast with typical Anglo-centric values such as autonomy, self-sufficiency and competitiveness. The African tradition of considering the 'we' rather than the 'I' in planning and decision-making fits in well with the interdependence and collaboration implicit in teamworking. Self-awareness and critical reflection on one's own team participation can help each team member play their role to the best of their ability and for the benefit of the team.

Case example

In a local authority Integrated Physical Disabilities Team, social workers, care managers from occupational therapy and nursing backgrounds, and health professionals were seeking to adopt a 'personalisation' approach to their work. Two team members attended training events and fed back information, providing the 'Specialist' team roles of disseminating knowledge and highlighting necessary skills to the rest of the team. Other team members obtained appropriate literature and internet sources for discussions at team meetings.

Two members contributed 'Plant' team roles, creatively and imaginatively promoting ways in which service users could be in control of the assessment, planning, intervention and review process, exercising choice and being active in designing their support packages. As the work developed, an issue for a number of service users was access to public transport and participation in community activities, leisure, sport and suitable work. A 'Resource Investigator' enthusiastically explored contacts with specialist voluntary organisations that opened up opportunities for service users. At one point, when a 'Shaper' challenged what she saw as too slow a pace of change and argued for the team to put pressure on management for changes in the system, a 'Teamworker' listened and acknowledged some of the areas where a change of culture in the organisation was needed but suggested more diplomatic ways to put forward proposals, thus averting friction. A 'Monitor Evaluator', weighing up options, suggested collection of data that would make a well-argued, accurate case to management for resources. At a team meeting, a 'Coordinator' chaired the discussion and helped the team clarify goals and agree plans of action. Several 'Implementers' were prominent in efficiently turning ideas into practical solutions.

This was an exciting time for the team. Morale was high and there was a feeling that they were empowering service users, using people skills and working in new and effective ways. In due course, the team manager pointed out that some accountability had slipped in the enthusiasm of working closely with service users. Some team members were not keeping regular detailed contact records, and there had been instances of practitioners dealing with service users when their designated worker was not available and not having the necessary details about recent contact and plans. Information sharing with GPs and other health professionals had also suffered. 'Completer Finishers' then took a more prominent role in diligently highlighting omissions and suggesting ways of balancing paper and computer work with service user involvement.

Team leadership

It is important to remember that a designated or functional team leader is also a team member with his or her own team role types and style. Leadership has traditionally been studied and written about focusing on:

- the personal qualities needed by a leader;
- the situations in which leaders find themselves;
- the actions that leaders need to take and the skills they require.

Personal qualities include personality characteristics and even appearance and physical makeup. However, it is difficult, if not impossible, to change these and the extent to which they influence leadership effectiveness is debatable. Situations can vary. One leader may cope well piloting a team through the resulting changes of a reorganisation or merger, while another might thrive as leader of a well-established interdisciplinary team. Personal qualities can be set and situations are often outside the leader's control but anyone finding themselves in a leadership position is responsible for their actions and can learn and develop skills.

Generally, leadership styles have been influenced by bureaucratic organisations that tend to have rigid structures and hierarchies modelled on the traditions of auto-cratic church government or military armies where commanding officers give orders. However, the management style of organisations and businesses has been shifting slowly over the years from command and control to advice and consent. The history of relationships between management and workers includes the setting up of a voluntary conciliation and arbitration service by government as far back as 1896. Through the development of various industrial relations, conciliation and advisory services, the independent Advisory, Conciliation and Arbitration Service (Acas) emerged, which became a statutory body in 1975.

Acas promotes moving away from hierarchies towards flexible, collaborative lead-ership that can adapt to change. A team leader cannot and should not escape functional authority and the accountability of the role, but is also entrusted with the responsibility to facilitate and enable teamworking. Hardingham and Royal (1994) suggested three 'start-up principles' highlighting important actions that leaders can take to make a team work effectively:

1. *Preparing individuals for team membership.* A leader can usefully see team members individually, listen to their ideas and clarify their roles and expectations.
2. *Ensuring 'baseline functioning'.* A leader can be influential in encouraging norms and procedures and agreeing ways of working. One of the roles of the team leader is to provide 'coaching' to individuals and to the team. It is interesting to note that the coach of an individual sportsperson or of a sports team is not a better performer than the individuals he or she coaches. The coach's skills and abilities involve developing the skills of others, challenging, encouraging, mentoring and working towards improving their performance.
3. *Agreeing objectives and performance measures.* Clear and challenging objectives need to be agreed by the team, and team leaders can play an important part in ensuring that all team members have contributed to goal setting. There also needs to be agreement on how the team will measure its own performance.

It is possible to be an extravert, outgoing ('Resource Investigator') leader or an introvert, reserved ('Complete Finisher') one. The outgoing person may find it easier to regularly and openly communicate with all team members but some may find such a person over-enthusiastic or intrusive. The more reserved team leader may find it easier to be reflective and give carefully considered answers but some might find that person slow or difficult to approach. Leaders have allowable weaknesses too! In their own personal style, leaders need to fully engage with their team members and enable them to play their team roles.

Functional leaders ought not be afraid to work with and encourage those team members who are providing leadership as part of their team roles, without being threatened by them. A leader can create tensions and lower morale by stifling innovation and ideas, expecting all team members to follow his or her style, not delegating and not acknowledging the valuable contributions that team members make.

Team membership

Being aware of one's own roles and accepting the team and functional roles of others is important for good team functioning. We have already noted that a team needs a variety of people playing different roles and contributing in different but complementary ways. In addition to 'baseline functioning' minimum expectations, it is helpful for team members to openly discuss and agree what is acceptable in terms of group processes, dynamics and relationships. The establishment of norms that lead to good performance is facilitated by an open, Adult-to-Adult style of communication and a supportive atmosphere where people are not afraid to take risks, say what they really think and develop one another's ideas. Conflict can be creative and is natural, human, unavoidable and can be managed leading to resolution. A team where everyone constantly agrees is probably not changing, developing and progressing.

In the management of any conflict between team members, an aim should be to avoid the confrontation situation that pits 'me' against 'you', my ideas against yours. A more productive stance is to consider how 'you' and 'me' in cooperation can work on a solution to the issue, problem or challenge facing us. The complexity of team interactions can be difficult to manage but, on a positive note, they also multiply the number of connections and exchanges to find solutions.

Team members can learn from experience, both successes and failures, what works well and what does not, by evaluating and reviewing performance. Teams need to meet regularly to assess their workload and circumstances facing them, plan ways forward and review progress. In active and effective teams, members work hard but also pay attention to more light-hearted aspects of life. Joint activities such as a coffee break, a meal or an agreed social event can enhance morale. Appropriate humour adds to the development of rapport. Members of effective teams achieve challenging objectives but enjoy themselves as they do so, leading to a sense of achievement.

There are sometimes simple but meaningful ways to contribute to the team, such as an agreement that individual members in rotation will share the chairing of team meetings. Offering to take the minutes of a meeting can be a welcome and valuable contribution.

New team members

Joining a team is an experience that requires learning and adjustment for the team as well as for the person joining it. There is formal information to absorb and informal norms to get to know. Healthy and honest communication between existing team members can be mirrored in how a new member is received. Maintaining a sense of openness and welcome helps an individual become a new member of a well-established team. An effective team is likely to be cohesive and close knit, which can make it more daunting to join and difficult for anyone new to feel a part of.

New team members need to get to know the policies, procedures and routines of the organisation and of the team and have to acquire information about internal and external facilities and resources. Open communication and answering questions before arrival can be very useful, as can be written and on-line information, which should be part of induction. New team members also need to become familiar with a team's culture, ethos and dynamics. These are less tangible factors and are not likely to be written down, but honest discussion about the team's life can be most helpful to a newcomer.

A test of a team's strength can be the way it welcomes new members. They bring experience, knowledge and skills and their own team roles that ideally will complement the roles of existing members. A new member can enhance the team but will inevitably change it. How flexible a team is and the permeability of its boundaries will have an effect on how comfortably it can accommodate newcomers. There can be a tendency, particularly in conforming and impermeable teams, to expect someone new to fit in with rigidly established procedures. The message is 'we have always done it this way, and we expect you to do it this way as well'. A mature but flexible team will accept that a new member can bring new ideas, questions and challenge, which can contribute to team development.

Reflection

Can you recall a time when you joined a new team or a new member joined a team of which you were a member?

- How did the team accept you or the other new member?
- What helped you or someone else join a new team?
- What was not helpful or hindered integration into a new team?
- How did you or another new member learn about organisational and team policies, procedures and routines?
- How did you or another new member discover the team culture, ethos and dynamics?

Boundaries of team membership

It is important to be clear about who are members of the team. Although it would appear straightforward, this is not always obvious and agreed by all concerned. Any team will have administrative needs and these are in some organisations managed centrally to service a number of teams. If there are secretaries, administrative and support staff that work for a team, particularly if they are physically located with the team, they are members of it and should be included in team meetings and other formal and informal activities. An organisational arrangement can sometimes be that line management for administrative and secretarial staff is separate from team operational management. However, it is important to be clear about the difference between line management as far as employment matters and conditions of service are concerned, and accountability to the team for work supporting professionals. Open communication and being kept informed of news and developments applies as much – if not more so – to support staff as to the professional practitioners within the team.

Some organisations, particularly local authorities, use agency supply workers when there are unfilled vacancies. Such appointments may be for a limited time due to, for instance, a full-time team member having maternity leave. Agency workers are team members and need to be included in all formal and informal team gatherings and interaction. There can be a feeling from colleagues that agency workers are not fully team members. Their pay is probably higher than that of other team members, their time with the team is limited and when they join a team they may find it difficult to 'hit the ground running' and quickly be conversant with team routines and culture. The more agency workers are included, the quicker they will feel part of the team and contribute to its life.

There may be professionals and other members of staff who work very closely with a team but who are members of another team within the organisation. This may apply to financial and administrative support, commissioning services and professional consultancy as might be provided by a local authority's principal social worker. It is advisable to have open lines of communication and information sharing with such individuals, regarding them as members of the 'extended team' and inviting them to team meetings, or for certain meeting agenda items, when appropriate.

Some administrative responsibilities might also be helpfully shared within a team. Social workers in a team will have their responsibilities towards service users and be engaged in the social work process of assessment, planning, intervention and review, but can helpfully contribute to the team by offering or agreeing to take on other tasks such as planning an event or being responsible for new allocations.

Emotional intelligence and resilience

We have already noted that human interaction is intrinsic to team collaboration and to the interdependence of team members. By definition, therefore, human emotions and feelings will be part of teamworking, particularly within the social work profession, which depends largely on human relationships to achieve its work. So it is important for team members to understand emotions, accurately appraise their emotional well-being, and manage feelings and emotions in an intelligent way.

Most psychologists have for some time accepted that there are probably a number of 'intelligences' that can be observed and to some extent measured, rather than conceptualising intelligence as one holistic phenomenon. I remember many years ago, before the concept of emotional intelligence (EI) was proposed, as a probation officer engaging with young offenders in an activity group that involved playing darts. Not only were they much better than me at throwing the darts and hitting required targets, they could also compute their score subtracting from 501 down and know what scores to aim for, including doubles and trebles, to reach zero with an amazing speed that left me far behind slowly working out the calculation in my mind. They did not have an academic or professional qualification but were far more 'intelligent' than me at darts technique and mental arithmetic. I hope I accepted my feelings of inferiority in keeping with EI, even though I was not familiar with the term at the time.

Early researchers in this field, Salovey and Mayer (1990: 189), defined emotional intelligence as 'the subset of social intelligence that involves the ability to monitor one's own and others' feelings and emotions, to discriminate among them and to use this information to guide one's thinking and actions'. Emotional intelligence, therefore, includes:

- *Perceiving emotions* in others (e.g. anger, frustration, excitement) and in ourselves as well as in paintings, sculpture, music, writing and other works of art and objects.
- *Understanding emotions*, emotional information and meaning, reasons for them, and the emotional content in human interaction and relationships.
- *Clear thinking*. Our emotional state and cognitive ability are closely bound, such as feeling we 'can't think straight' when we are stressed, so being aware of our emotions and managing them helps us to reason and be objective.
- *Managing emotions*. Being open to feelings and responding appropriately enables us to act logically and objectively as a professional while acknowledging the emotional content of our interactions.

In a review of EI research and its application of it to social work, Morrison (2007: 251) suggests that different writers agree on the interrelatedness of four constituents of EI, two intrapersonal and two interpersonal:

Interpersonal intelligence	Intrapersonal intelligence
Self-awareness	Other awareness
Self-management	Relationship management

Writing about the importance of EI for social workers, Howe (2008: 1) stated:

> It is critical that social and health care workers understand the fundamental part that emotions play in the lives and behavior of those who use their service. Emotions define the character of the professional relationship. Practitioners need to understand how emotions affect them as they work with users and engage with colleagues.

Morrison (2007) explored the relevance of EI to engagement, assessment and observation, decision-making, and collaboration and cooperation. Relating to the latter, he points out that emotion is an expression of individual, collective and institutional experience. He argues that

> it is possible to see how individuals' feelings and relationship capacities are intertwined with the emotional needs and rules of the organisation in its struggle for survival. Thus, problematic micro-level interactions between staff often act out unspoken macro-level tensions within and between organisations.
>
> (Morrison, 2007: 257)

Since being emotionally literate helps people achieve goals in life and work, even when circumstances would suggest negative outcomes, a related concept is *emotional resilience*. Individuals who achieve a good work/life balance, look after their physical and mental health, manage their time as part of managing stress, and feel positive and enthusiastic about their work are better placed to deal with difficult events, emergencies and change – that is, they are more resilient.

Teams can enhance the emotional resilience of members and may have an emotional resilience of their own. Team resilience involves aspects of teamworking that we have already considered, including:

- good, open communication;
- interdependence and collaboration;
- appreciating each others' contributions, which enhances the self-esteem of individual team members;
- mutual support and managing stress;
- balancing hard work with enjoyable social events;
- anticipating busy and difficult times and preparing for them.

Self-leadership

Earlier in this chapter we explored team leadership as a functional, or designated, role and the leadership to which all team members can contribute through their team roles and mutual support. The leadership of others involves influencing, facilitating and enabling colleagues to achieve agreed goals. Self-leadership involves self-awareness and self-management, setting personal goals, using emotional intelligence, being self-critical and learning from mistakes in a process of influencing, facilitating and enabling oneself to succeed in life and work. Neck and Manz (2012) argue that self-leadership is a precursor for the effective leadership of others.

Self-leadership could mistakenly be seen as self-seeking and egocentric. However, it involves succeeding through collaborating with others including learning to be a good team member. So team membership involves emotional intelligence and self-leadership. A team can benefit from motivated and determined individuals who engage in continuous professional development and whose goals may include eventual promotion. Good team members remain interdependent, playing complementary roles and working collaboratively towards a common purpose to achieve agreed results. In such ways, they are accountable to the team for their participation in it. A team member who selfishly pursues their own goals is not contributing to agreed aims and objectives and the achievement of team tasks.

Chapter summary

Having focused on the whole team as an entity in the previous chapter, the focus of this chapter has been on the individuals that come together to form a team and what they contribute to it. Consideration of the characteristics of team members led us to explore the different but complementary roles that they play. The chapter highlighted the difference between functional roles, dependent on a person's job title and description, and team roles – what individuals contribute to the team through their personality and behaviour. We explored Belbin's team roles taking account of their strengths and positive contribution to the team, and their 'allowable weaknesses'.

The chapter briefly considered team leadership with a reminder that the designated team leader is also a member of the team; that leadership can be a functional and a team role; and that leadership can be helpfully shared among team members. An exploration of other aspects of team membership and interaction among team members led to consider the importance of how new members are welcomed and integrated into a team. The chapter also considered boundaries of team membership, pointing out that administrative, secretarial and other support staff can and should be regarded as members of the team even if their line management is outside the team or if some belong to other teams within the organisation.

The latter part of the chapter focused on our individual emotional intelligence, emotional resilience and self-leadership. We noted that emotional intelligence includes being aware of emotions in others and in ourselves as well as in other aspects of life, understanding and managing emotions in a way that helps us to reason and be objective. We saw that individuals who accomplish a good work/life balance, look after their physical and mental health, manage their time and stress, and are optimistic about their work are better placed to deal with difficult events, emergencies and change (i.e. they are emotionally resilient). We acknowledged that a team can be emotionally resilient.

Lastly, the chapter explored self-leadership, involving personal goal setting, using emotional intelligence, being self-aware and self-critical, and learning from mistakes to encourage personal success in life and work. This was seen not as self-seeking and egocentric but involving collaboration with others including learning to be a good team member.

Further reading

Belbin, R.M. (2010) *Team Roles at Work*, 2nd edn. Oxford: Butterworth-Heinemann. In addition to outlining the original research and how Team Role theory developed, this textbook has chapters on 'Interpersonal chemistry in the workplace', 'Managing difficult working relationships' and 'A strategy for self-management'.

Howe, D. (2008) *The Emotionally Intelligent Social Worker*. Basingstoke: Palgrave Macmillan. This textbook outlines what emotional intelligence is and applies it to social work. It explores emotional development and working with emotions, in relation to both service users and colleagues.

5 Teamworking skills

Introduction

Although the whole of this textbook addresses topics relating to skills needed for effective teamworking, this chapter more specifically reviews the particular skills and personal qualities necessary for social workers to participate successfully as team members.

As a practitioner, you will have a set of social work skills discussed by various textbooks. In a helpful review, Trevithick (2012) includes skills in communication, observation, listening and assessment, interviewing, providing help, direction and guidance, empowerment, negotiation and partnership skills, and professional competence and accountability. Many of these are transferable and relevant to interacting with colleagues and other professionals in teamworking. You are also likely to have specialist skills that you bring to the team. These are often related to communicating and working with specific service user groups. You may also have other related and relevant skills such as IT, organisational ability, or a second language.

Social work now has a Professional Capabilities Framework (PCF) (The College of Social Work, 2012). Although social work practice is best understood holistically through the framework that consists of nine interdependent capabilities, in exploring skills relevant to teamworking this chapter will refer to some of the specific PCF domains. The underpinning foundation offered by the PCF provides a common base – or steer – from entry to social work right up to senior positions. Teamwork is an activity experienced by social work students (see Chapter 9) and throughout a social worker's career. The concept of capability suggests an individual's potential to develop to a certain level of competence rather than regarding a person as either competent or not.

The skills explored below are not all exclusive to teamworking, as many are used by individual social workers in other aspects of their work. However, it is useful to review them here in the context of teamworking, although it is difficult to highlight skills in isolation without paying attention to the development of a team ethos within which skills are practised, the personal qualities of a practitioner and an underpinning professional value base. Nevertheless, this chapter focuses mainly on individual skills.

Communication skills

In communication with colleagues and other professionals individually, in groups and in meetings it is important to engage, concentrate, make sure we hear what others are saying and pay full attention to them. In open plan and other busy office settings, it is easy to be distracted and miss all or some of what people are telling us due to competing background noise. For sensitive conversations and discussions, it is advisable to make arrangements to go somewhere where there is privacy and no interruptions.

Reflection

Think of meetings you have attended, whether involving a small number of people or the whole team.

- Did everyone show full attention all of the time?
- If so, what made you aware that they were paying attention when they were not speaking?
- If not, what made you aware that some individuals were not paying attention? How did that make you feel?

Non-verbal communication is important. Our physical position when talking to someone or in a meeting can indicate involvement. Adopting an open, non-defensive posture can be a sign that you are open to others. Good eye contact and the give-and-take of dialogue help make a connection. Active listening responses, including apparently negligible ones such as nods of the head and 'minimal encouragers', such as 'mmm . . .' and 'yes' can indicate interest when face-to-face with someone, on the telephone or in a meeting, particularly during a period when you are not contributing verbally. Seeking clarification, checking understanding and summarising content at appropriate points are also all part of active listening. Interrupting others or finishing their sentences suggests that you are not fully listening or that you are impatient, rather than showing that you are so in tune with what they are telling you that you can say it for them.

The skills of being able to challenge others and giving and receiving feedback are part of teamwork interaction. Appropriately questioning the ideas of others during team debate and discussion can lead to a full exploration of issues. When giving feedback to others, particularly in a team setting, it is best to be factual, giving examples, avoiding emotional overtones or judgemental remarks, and to refer to the behaviour and actions of those to whom you are giving feedback, not to them as a person. You are commenting on what they have done, not who they are. Be specific in your feedback, avoiding generalisations. Ask for and welcome feedback on yourself, listening carefully to it and accepting it non-defensively. Ask questions to clarify information and treat it as constructive criticism.

The use of email is commonplace in our modern lifestyle to communicate between friends and relatives and at work. The increased use of email in social work today follows the trend of most workplaces. Its use for communicating within a team has advantages and disadvantages. It is a quick means of keeping everyone informed and of exchanging views. Emails can contribute to team cohesion and development when used for appropriate encouragement, thanks for mutual help and to share relevant reading material that a practitioner may have come across such as an article relevant to the team in a social work journal.

However, there is a need to follow email etiquette and be courteous and professional. Do check your email regularly and answer promptly those that need a reply. You should be careful about the content of an email and observe confidentiality, taking into account the trail of emails that preceded the one you are sending, which can be deleted if necessary, and how many people are copied in on it. There is a danger that individuals can vent strong immediate feelings of annoyance or frustration quickly and send this to all members of a team when some pause for thought and reflection might result in a more considered and acceptable message being transmitted. Open arguments on email are distracting and can create resentment.

It is important to be professional in other forms of written communication. Although this is a skill that is part of social work in general, it has particular implications for teamwork, which involves routinely communicating in writing. If your records are up to date, succinct and clear, fellow team members are able to look them up when answering a telephone query or seeing a service user that has called at the team office when you are not there. Teams are occasionally involved in the preparation of particular proposals and plans in written reports requesting resources or contributing to organisational policy. These need to be well constructed and argued, reflecting the views of the whole team. A high standard of writing makes it more likely that the communication will be effective.

Interpersonal relationships and collaboration

As a social work practitioner, you will be engaging with other team members in Adult-to-Adult transactions, being honest, open and objective, particularly if dealing with differences of professional opinion. Debate and disagreement within a team is healthy if conducted politely, focusing on issues rather than personalities. Teamworking involves collaborating, interacting and connecting with others. The analogy of sports teams can provide helpful parallels. In teams such as basketball, netball, football and rugby, with a range of five to thirteen players on the field, individuals have different roles and a game plan, know their positions, are interdependent and collaborate with one another with the aim of achieving a winning result. An egocentric individual who attempts to score points personally is not enhancing the team. A team player contributes their skills and experience and sacrifices some of their own personal recognition and power for the benefit of the team.

There are other models of sport teams. In a national tennis team in an international competition, a single player or pairs of individuals take part in matches. However, those separate results contribute to the standing of the overall team. In a relay track or swimming event, individuals execute their segment to the best of their ability handing over smoothly to a team-mate when they have played their part. In world championships or at Olympic Games, each country enters a 'team' but it comprises a variety of individuals and groups that specialise in diverse sports. These might be models of collaboration applicable to interdisciplinary or multi-agency teams that are geographically scattered but nevertheless work towards a common purpose – that of supporting and helping service users and carers.

In addition to collaboration, other skills are listed below that are needed in particular to manage differences of opinion or conflict. These skills are involved in pursuing the styles of responding to conflict outlined in Chapter 3.

- *Cooperation* – acknowledging the goals of other professionals or colleagues rather than focusing on personal or individual agency ones. This involves working with others and offering to help if needed.
- *Disclosure* – being open about the ideas and feelings of others, voicing our own, and entering into discussion and debate rather than adopting a closed position.
- *Flexibility* – the willingness to confront and move to resolve conflict rather than being inflexible.
- *Participation* – engaging with others and being active in conflict resolution rather than withdrawn.

The development of interpersonal relationships and collaboration extends, as suggested by some sport analogies, to working with professionals in other organisations. This will be explored further in Chapter 8. Suffice to say here that getting to know and building working relationships with practitioners in other agencies is crucial to inter-professional collaboration. This networking with others enhances the team that can be built around the service user.

Assertiveness skills are significant to effective interpersonal relationships within teams. Assertiveness can be visualised as the mid-point of a behaviour continuum where at one extreme there are passive and submissive individuals and at the opposite end forceful and aggressive ones. Passive individuals tend to agree to and submit unquestioningly to any requests and to the wishes of others as a helpless Adapted Child in transactional analysis, responding to a demanding Controlling Parent. The result of their behaviour is that they feel disempowered. Forceful individuals expect to get their own way, misuse power and egocentrically focus on their own needs as a Controlling Parent, expecting the obedience of an inferior Adapted Child.

Hargie and Dickson (2004: 309) suggest that 'in order to execute assertiveness skills effectively, three central components need to be mastered: content, process and nonverbal responses.' In the *content* of their interaction, assertive individuals are able to deal with emotionally charged issues by acknowledging the feelings of others but remaining objective, focusing on factual information and relating to others in an Adult-to-Adult way. In the interpersonal *process* between them and others, assertive individuals avoid ambiguity and hidden agendas, free of 'games' such as those inherent in 'drama triangle' cycle transactions. They are able to be firm but fair and remain calm when there are heated arguments. The *non-verbal responses* of assertive individuals correspond with those outlined above and convey attention, interest and a non-defensive, appropriately self-confident stance.

Qualities based on professional social work values

Traditional 'Rogerian' qualities are not only beneficial for relationship-based work with service users, they also underpin the effective interaction between team members that has been outlined thus far in this chapter. Rogers (1961) outlined three personal qualities essential to a person-centred approach in relationships: empathy, unconditional positive regard and self-congruence. Here they are applied to teamwork.

Empathy is the understanding of another team member's concerns as if you were them, rather than relating their issues to your frame of reference and perceiving them from your point of view. Active listening skills can be used to check that your empathetic understanding is genuine and captures the essence of what they wish to communicate. *Unconditional positive regard* is the basic acceptance of another team member as a person without judging what they are saying or doing. This approach is conducive to the development of trust and partnership. It involves respecting others even if we disagree with them. *Self-congruence* is achieved when our ideal self (the person we would like to be) matches our actual self (the person we are). The need for self-awareness is important in this respect if our self-image is to be in line with how other team members perceive us. Self-congruence makes us genuine or 'real' to others.

Such qualities are in harmony with professional social work ethical principles and values such as being non-judgemental, having respect for others and accepting diversity. The second of the PCF domains – Values and Ethics (The College of Social Work, 2012) – suggests that as social workers we should be capable of managing our own values, understanding and applying the ethics and values of the profession to ethical reasoning and ethical dilemmas, respecting confidentiality and promoting partnership. All these expectations resonate with the collaboration and cooperation between team members necessary for effective teamworking

The pursuit of value-based qualities requires self-awareness. We noted as part of good communication skills that in playing one's role within the team it is healthy to behave in an open and honest way. The more self-congruent and genuine we are, the less likely it is that our responses will be cluttered by unconscious processes, reflect the transference of negative feelings and be guarded by defence mechanisms. Value-based characteristics become part of the person we are, enabling us to naturally and automatically engage in behaviour that others find helpful and amiable rather than negative and cautious.

Professionalism

Activity

What does being professional mean to you? Write down your immediate thoughts without looking up dictionary or textbook definitions.

The term 'professional' tends to be used in different ways and you will have written down your own thoughts about this. To you or others it might mean someone who has a professional qualification, not an amateur, competent, registered with a professional regulator, working to a high standard of practice, reliable.

The first of the PCF domains – Professionalism (The College of Social Work, 2012) – lists expectations such as identifying and behaving as a professional social worker, committed to professional development. The domain also includes professional demeanour, managing personal and professional boundaries, use of self, emotional resilience and being accountable.

Being organised, reliable and having good verbal and written communication skills, as previously mentioned, are part of being professional. Reliability is significant to teamwork because it has an impact on other team members. If others can 'count on' you to take on your fair share of the team's workload and consistently deliver what you have agreed to do, the effectiveness of the team as a whole, and its morale, will be strengthened.

'Demeanour' includes conduct, behaviour and deportment. In inter-professional work, when teamworking with professionals of other disciplines and agencies, it is important to respect, not be intimidated by and have a comparable level of professionalism to that of any other practitioner. It can be easy to displace personal feelings onto professional interaction within and without the team. This leads to a blurring of personal and professional boundaries.

An aspect of professionalism that helps your own development is being aware of the meso and macro contexts within which social work teams operate. Knowing your organisation allows you to find channels to influence and contribute to organisational policy and practice, which will be discussed further in the next chapter. It is also important to keep up to date with government policy, initiatives and legislation. Having an informed outlook and the ability to see the 'bigger picture', beyond your immediate working environment, gives you an objective perspective and enhances your wider understanding of issues.

We have already noted in previous chapters the extent to which the interdependence of team members results in feelings and emotions being part of teamworking interaction. Emotional intelligence and resilience, as discussed in Chapter 4, requires individuals to identify, assess and work with one's own emotions, those of others and, collectively, those of the whole team. Our thinking and actions can be guided by our awareness of the feelings and emotions of others and by our assessment of how those emotions are affecting them. Understanding the emotional content of interaction helps us to maintain professional boundaries. Emotional resilience leads us to plan our individual goals, thus enhancing our personal and professional development.

Self-management and personal organisational skills

Time and workload management are fundamental skills needed by all professionals. It is useful for individuals to consider how important any task is and, as a separate consideration, how urgent it is. Deciding how central the task is to an individual's purpose, aims and goals determines its importance. Completing a continuous professional development portfolio due in six months' time is important to enhance the professionalism of an individual social worker, but is not urgent until the submission date becomes much nearer. Urgency is dependent on how soon a task has to be completed. A Court report due in one or two days time is urgent.

Understanding the difference between importance and urgency helps individuals plan for important tasks that are not yet urgent; prioritise urgent tasks whose deadline is approaching; deal as speedily as possible with routine 'quick and simple' tasks that are urgent but not important; spend the least amount of time possible on 'time wasters' that are neither important nor urgent; and avoid crises created by failing to tackle important tasks until they become urgent.

Activity

List some of your tasks in the four quadrants below:

High Importance

Priorities/Crises	Planning

High Urgency | | | Low Urgency

Quick and simple	Time wasters

Low Importance

There are extra dimensions to consider when the organisation of each team member is part of how time and workload is managed by a team. Matters regarded as important by each individual may not be the most important for the team. It is necessary to discuss the importance of team priorities by focusing on the team's purpose, aims and objectives. A team benefits from regularly discussing the urgency of tasks facing it, agreeing plans and setting goals towards completion. There also needs to be agreement on who will undertake tasks to achieve goals and an awareness of each others' workloads when discussing who can take on additional responsibilities and accept work being allocated to them.

Activity

List some of your team's tasks in the four quadrants below:

High Importance

Priorities/Crises	**Planning**
Quick and simple	**Time wasters**

High Urgency　　　　　　　　　　　　　　　　　　　**Low Urgency**

Low Importance

What are the similarities and differences? How do these tasks compare to the ones you listed earlier focusing on your individual time management?

The balance between active interaction resulting in buzz and energy within the team, and informal talk or gossip that detracts from the efficiency of teamworking, can be difficult to achieve. On a day-to-day basis, the interface between members within a team is positive when focused and purposeful but can result in interruptions and time wasting.

Reflection

Think of your daily routine.

- How do you spend your time when you are at your workplace?
- What is the balance between working at your desk, writing, using the computer, having discussions with others, chatting, taking breaks, attending meetings?
- Do you plan your day (e.g. with a 'to do' list) and accomplish what you set out to do, or do you spend a lot of time reacting to unexpected requests, interactions and interruptions?

There are specific behaviours that you can adopt when others come to talk to you, particularly in an open plan office:

- stick to the point and keep it short;
- continue to look busy;
- stand up;
- be assertive – tell the person honestly that you do not have time to talk right now; if possible arrange with someone who has come to see you to meet later;
- visit your interrupter, you are then in control;
- consider using other means of communication – telephone, email, memos, notes.

You can make yourself unavailable at certain times by booking a quiet room or working at home if acceptable. Let others in the team know about this and indicate when you will be available.

Full workloads and heavy schedules can result in stress. It is helpful to identify your sources of stress, both at a personal level and those related to work. You may be tempted to blame others and outside events but it is healthy to consider to what extent your stress is within your own control and the result of how you perceive stress within you. Until we accept some responsibility for our own part in deciding what is stressful to us and maintaining a stressful lifestyle, stress will remain outside our control. Planning and prioritising work helps manage stress. Discussion of workloads and stress within a team helps share and minimise it. Assertiveness and time and workload management are part of managing stress.

Critical reflection and analysis

The sixth PCF domain – Critical Reflection and Analysis (The College of Social Work, 2012) – is described as the capability to 'Apply critical reflection and analysis to inform and provide a rationale for professional decision-making'. It includes the use of critical thinking, using multiple sources of knowledge and evidence, applying creativity and curiosity, creating hypotheses and putting forward a rationale for judgements and decisions.

Professional decision-making is expected of social workers. Within a team, members can explore problems using a problem-solving approach and then proceed to make a decision, which ideally will be agreed by all team members. Team discussion is useful to define problems (what is a problem for one team member may not be so for others and what is a problem for the organisation's management may not be a problem for the team), generate alternative responses, evaluate and select a way forward and agree how to implement solutions.

Decision-making involves clear thinking and exploring alternatives to select a course of action. A SWOT analysis (listing the Strengths, Weaknesses or limitations, Opportunities and Threats of a way forward) can be a useful strategic planning tool. The decision-making process requires a final decision choice or cut-off point. Reaching this stage is a discipline that teams do well to pursue. Sometimes for urgent matters that require a quick decision and swift response, there may not always be time to have a full team discussion and teams must accept this. The team should nevertheless be kept informed of such decisions. The difference between urgency and importance outlined above is relevant here. Important decisions relating to the team's purpose, aims and objectives should ideally be reached through a more democratic approach involving full team discussion. Teams have at times to acknowledge however that democracy can be time-consuming and some team members may find a slow decision-making process frustrating. This in itself can be a source of tension.

Team decisions are not without problems. The concept of synergy suggests that decisions made by a cohesive group of people are more effective than those made independently by any of the individuals in the group. It can be argued that decisions made by a group of individuals collectively are different to those that might be made by any of the members of the group because group dynamics result in the decision being the responsibility of the group, not of any one individual. The phenomenon of 'groupthink' proposed by the psychologist Irving Janis studying examples of US military incorrect decisions, applies to a situation where a group makes a flawed decision because group pressure leads to a weakening of 'mental efficiency, reality testing, and moral judgement' (Janis, 1972: 9). It would appear that such decisions lack critical reflection and full analysis, so it is imperative that teams pursue this in their discussions. When meeting with other professionals, it is important for disquiet to be voiced and risks to be explored. It is common for concerns to be minimised or glossed over in a meeting only for individuals to raise them later by telephone or email.

Participating in meetings and planning

Part of effective teamworking involves regular team meetings with a set agenda that is distributed in advance. Your involvement and participation includes contributing appropriate items for the agenda. It is helpful for these to be issues that require team discussion rather than trivial queries, minor items of information or complaints. Members of the team can share chairing meetings. Participation also involves coming to team meetings prepared, having read papers circulated in advance, listening to others in discussion and putting forward your views. It is important to minute action points and review them at the next meeting.

In addition to meetings where routine business matters concerning the running of the team are discussed, it is appropriate sometimes to devote a substantial amount of time at a regular meeting, or agree a special meeting, to planning, reflection or to discuss work with service users and other topics of interest to the team.

Some meetings can benefit from the use of a flipchart or a whiteboard if available. Issues to be explored can be put up at the start of the meeting and added to as discussion develops with suggestions and actions also included. Post-it™ notes can be effective for discussion of team objectives, for instance. They allow for objectives to be written up and placed in order of importance as they are discussed. Post-it™ notes of a different colour can be used in a similar way to agree and prioritise tasks that need to be done to achieve the objectives and who will undertake them.

A related technique is to have three flipcharts or columns on a white board with planning headings such as 'Backlog', 'To do' and 'Done'. Post-it™ notes can be used for items under these headings and these can be moved around and added to as priorities are discussed and progress reviewed. The interaction by team members through this exercise can be as beneficial as the results of the planning.

Skills checklist

Consider the skills below, relating them to your participation in teamworking. Look them up in the chapter for more detail of what they involve.

	Rate your capability for each skill on a scale of 1 (poor) to 5 (capable)	Plan ways of developing skills for which you have scored yourself low
Communication skills		
Communicating verbally		
Communicating non-verbally		
Attending		
Actively listening		
Challenging others		
Giving feedback		
Seeking and accepting feedback		
Using email constructively		
Communicating effectively in writing		
Interpersonal relationships and collaboration		
Interacting		
Engaging		
Connecting		
Debating openly		
Talking through disagreements		
Being objective		
Collaborating		
Cooperation		
Disclosure		
Flexibility		
Participation		
Networking		
Being assertive		
Qualities based on social work values		
Empathy		

Unconditional positive regard		
Self-congruence		
Ethical reasoning		
Promoting partnership		
Self-awareness		
Professionalism		
Being organised		
Reliability		
Professional demeanour		
Managing personal and professional boundaries		
Awareness of meso and macro contexts affecting the team		
Knowing your organisation		
Keeping up to date with national developments and legislation		
Emotional intelligence		
Emotional resilience		
Self-management and personal organisational skills		
Managing time and workload		
Planning		
Prioritising		
Contributing to team workload management		
Managing interruptions		
Managing stress		
Critical reflection and analysis		
Problem-solving		
Decision-making		
Avoiding 'groupthink'		
Weighing up concerns and risks		
Participating in meetings and planning		
Contributing meeting agenda items		
Chairing meetings		
Participating in meetings		
Using planning techniques		

Chapter summary

Although it is difficult to highlight skills in isolation of a team ethos, personal qualities of team members and their underpinning professional value base, this chapter has focused on teamworking skills. Even though social work practice is best understood holistically through the Professional Capabilities Framework (PCF) that consists of nine interdependent capabilities, this chapter has referred to some of the specific PCF domains.

In keeping with the interaction, interdependence and cooperation inherent in teamworking, this chapter reviewed verbal and non-verbal and written communication skills, those needed for interpersonal relationships and collaboration, and the personal qualities of empathy, unconditional positive regard and self-congruence based on professional social work values.

The chapter used two PCF domains – Professionalism and Critical Reflection and Analysis – as headings to explore further skills. To these were added a more individual approach through considering self-management and personal organisation skills in the context of teamworking. The chapter concluded by exploring practical skills necessary for participating in meetings and planning. A final 'skills checklist' provided a record of the skills reviewed and a self-assessment tool.

Further reading

Hargie, O. and Dickson, D. (2004) *Skilled Interpersonal Communication: Research, Theory and Practice*. Hove: Routledge. Although not a social work textbook, the authors provide a thorough exploration of interpersonal communication and relationship skills, review some skills relevant to self-management and offer a final chapter on 'Groups and group interaction' that includes the advantages of group cohesion and team characteristics.

Thompson, N. (2009) *People Skills*, 3rd edn. Basingstoke: Palgrave Macmillan. Written as a guide for those involved in 'people professions', this textbook considers the importance of personal effectiveness skills and skills involved in personal interactions. It includes a chapter on multidisciplinary working.

PART 2
Applying teamworking skills in practice

PART 2
Applying teamworking skills
in practice

6 Working in organisations

Introduction

Earlier chapters introduced teamworking (Chapter 2), explored teams as holistic entities (Chapter 3) and team membership (Chapter 4), including a number of underpinning theoretical ideas and professional values. The previous chapter (Chapter 5) focused on the skills required for teamworking. We now apply more specifically what we have been considering to practice situations, or put the previous considerations into a practice context.

The eighth PCF domain – Contexts and Organisations (The College of Social Work, 2012) – is explained as 'Engage with, inform and adapt to changing contexts that shape practice. Operate effectively within own organisational frameworks and contribute to the development of services and organisations. Operate effectively within multi-agency and inter-professional settings.' It includes:

- Knowing your organisation.
- Knowing your role and responsibilities.
- Contributing to organisational policy and practice.
- Working with other people/professionals.
- Team working.
- Working with other organisations.
- Working with changing contexts.

This is a daunting list of expectations. They apply to all social workers and in this chapter we explore implications of these capabilities, in particular as they relate to teamworking. We noted in Chapter 2 and elsewhere that it helps to understand teamwork if one puts it into wider meso and macro contexts. The next two chapters will discuss the application of teamworking skills to multidisciplinary teams and to inter-professional collaboration. Here, we consider various aspects of working within your organisation and how teams fit into that setting.

Teams in organisations

Organisations employing social workers range from large bureaucratic local authorities to small private agencies. In recent years, social work has experienced the 'managerialism' of directives, standards, procedures, targets, quality and budget controls, and accountability. Although many of these originate from central government, individual social workers can feel that 'the organisation' is a disconnected or remote entity, difficult to relate to, let alone influence. There may have been times when you have perceived your organisation, or its senior management, as not helpful in getting the professional best out of you or other individuals. It feels as if the organisation makes demands, sets at times unrealistic expectations and controls practitioners rather than facilitating and enabling professional originality and vision. Reorganisations and restructuring are a regular feature of the management of social work and, while they seldom achieve their stated aims, they add to a sense of instability and transient structures.

Where does teamworking fit into all this? Collectively, teams may at times also feel unsupported by managerial systems but they can be a vehicle for social workers to engage positively with the organisation and to contribute to organisational policy and practice. This chapter will take an optimistic view of what is possible if you get to know your organisation and find effective ways to work within it, accepting that this involves working within ever changing contexts.

Payne (2000: 170) suggests 'four approaches to thinking about the structure of teamwork in and between organisations'. These are a 'link pin structure', 'matrix structures', 'systems approaches' and 'network approaches'.

Within an organisation's hierarchy there may be a senior management team, operational teams responsible for specific services and work teams that will include social workers. A *link pin structure* reminds us that the team leader (or another representative) of a work team will also be a member of an operational team further up the hierarchy, while a manager from an operational team will also be a member of the senior management team further up the hierarchy. Thus there are 'link pin' individuals who provide a connection between teams by being a member of one or more of them within the organisational structure. They are crucial to line management accountability and their responsibility is to cascade information downwards and represent the view of their teams up the hierarchy of an organisation.

This is, of course, a way of thinking about teams in organisations in a rather rigid and set framework, not allowing for the complexities of power dynamics and the personalities of individuals involved. People in organisations will engage in informal communication outside lines of official accountability. Nevertheless, to achieve formal influence as a social worker you need to know your organisational structure and who the 'link pins' are and use participation in your team to make responses to communications sent down the hierarchy and to prepare well-argued proposals when appropriate that can be put forward through line management. You may also suggest that a 'link pin' or other appropriate line manager attend agreed team meetings for discussion of proposals, resources, current issues and concerns. Through these activities you will develop skills to influence your organisation.

Specific project or planning teams are at times set up using individuals from a number of different teams and levels in an organisation, and on occasion from other organisations. In these *matrix structures*, individuals of different positions, jobs or levels within the organisation, or from different organisations and disciplines, come together as a team for a specific purpose with a clear remit. Connexions, Youth Offending Teams and Community Mental Health Teams may be seen as examples of permanent matrix teams. However, matrix teams sometimes come together for a limited, relatively short time to work on a specific assignment. To engage with and contribute to your organisation, you can volunteer to be part of such teams or ensure you are aware of their existence and how they operate so that you are able to contribute or receive information and suggestions. Skills involved in networking within your organisation, discussed further below, also relate to matrix structures and enable you to influence your organisation.

Owing to the complexity of human interaction, an organisation can be envisaged as an interconnected 'living organism' such as the human body or a family (or a central heating system). Another analogy for these concepts, discussed in Chapter 2, is that of 'ecological' systems in nature. Payne (2000: 172) describes *systems approaches* in organisations, suggesting that:

> Teams are seen as spheres of influence, with boundaries. Where boundaries overlap there are flows of influence through communication, joint working or shared interests. The influence may be overlapping membership, or represent groupings of interests. Where teams share many cases, for example, you might see overlapping interests.

These 'teams' may be more fluid and informal than others thus far considered. A negative view is that they include gossip and rumour spheres of influence. A more positive approach that you can take is to be aware of such approaches and be part of communication and shared interest systems. Examples might include discussion groups focusing on social work topics and a Black workers support group. These can contribute to a 'community of practice' and 'learning organisation', discussed below.

Network approaches use the many links and connections within and outside of the organisation (like an internet web). Networking is a means of tapping into the skills and knowledge of individuals within the organisation and external contacts. An 'eco map' with you or your team in the centre can depict radiating lines of contact that can 'specify the amount and nature of the relationships within and between different groups' (Payne, 2000: 175). Networking skills add another device to your 'tool box' for working in organisations.

Case example

A Youth Offending Team (YOT) organised an evening information giving and networking event for local authority committee members, officers, local judiciary and other stakeholders that included refreshments and the opportunity to join 'stalls' run by members of the team to exchange views and receive information on YOT activities, such as bail and remand support, intensive resettlement, reparation, parenting sessions and work with volunteers.

Members of the team contributed to the various aspects of organising, publicising and running the event, in addition to their current work responsibilities, but saw it as an investment of time that would result in influential people being better informed and more aware of YOT work, supporting future developments and enabling the team to obtain new resources.

To '[o]perate effectively within your own organisational frameworks and contribute to the development of services and organisations' (The College of Social Work, 2012), you can make use of formal and informal networks and you need to be aware of channels of communication and accountability within organisational structures and line management. As stated before, you will also benefit from understanding teamwork within wider meso and macro systemic contexts.

Organisational and team culture

Reflection
- To what extent are you interested in other cultures? This may be through going on holidays abroad, reading, or due to the nationality and ethnic mix of your family and friends.
- What are the elements that make up the 'culture' of another country or part of the world that you can experience and learn more about?

In your reflection you may have included elements such as customs, traditions, language, climate, identity, myths, ceremonies and values. When considering an organisational or team culture, we focus on similar concepts within work settings.

Organisations and teams have:

- customs and traditions;
- verbal and written communication and jargon;
- a climate or morale that can vary and be higher or lower depending on internal and external pressures and changes;
- an identity put forward through logos, strap lines and mission statements;
- myths that include reminiscing, rumours and gossip;
- ceremonies at times of farewell and celebrations;
- values, beliefs and attitudes.

One would expect that professional social work values will influence the culture of social work agencies resulting in accepting service users and staff non-judgementally and providing a person-centred service. Of course, organisational culture is the combined behaviour and habits of humans that form the organisation. Individuals contribute to the organisational culture and in turn their behaviour, attitudes, thinking and feelings are influenced by the culture of the organisation.

Teams also have a culture, ethos and traditional ways of doing things, which influence and are influenced by the organisational culture. This includes approaches to thinking about the structure of teamwork in and between organisations. We saw in Chapter 4 that when a new member joins a team, in addition to getting to know policies and procedures, they need to tune into the more intangible team culture and norms. They can benefit from discussion with and mentoring from the team's prominent 'culture carriers' who can explain traditions, habits, what is considered acceptable and how things are done beyond official procedural systems. The culture of effective teams includes team members' agreement on its purpose and challenging goals, open communication, trust, collaboration, mutual support, shared leadership and learning from experience. To work within and contribute to such a team culture, the teamworking skills highlighted in the previous chapter are needed.

Service user and carer participation

Professional social work values, policy and practice, and the capability to work with other people, must embrace the involvement of people who use services and carers and enable their full participation in all aspects of service provision. Wright et al. (2006) proposed a whole systems approach to developing service user and carer participation. It involves four interdependent areas that an organisation should develop: a culture, structure, effective practice and effective review systems.

A culture and ethos that demonstrates an organisation's commitment to participation needs to be shared by all staff, service users and carers, and should be apparent in information and written communication, how service users and carers are talked about, can access premises, are welcomed and their physical presence accepted in work areas. There are meetings, such as reviews, where attendance and participation by service users, family and carers must be the norm. In addition, a telling measure of a team culture that supports service user involvement would be to note whether people who use services and carers are not only mentioned but are continually the focus of discussions at team meetings.

An organisation's infrastructures should show evidence of planning, developing and resourcing the participation of service users and carers. In addition, service users and carers themselves will be actively and meaningfully involved in the plans, developments and decisions about resources in organisations whose structure supports their participation. A challenge is for this to be evident also at team level.

In organisations that support service user and carer participation, their full involvement will be evident in practice. This may be seen at different levels, including participation in their own assessment, planning, intervention and review; involvement in the recruitment and selection of new staff; and being consulted about an organisation's policies, procedures and standards. Within teams, a variety of ways of working, methods for participation, skills and knowledge will enable people who use the services and carers to become involved.

Service user and carer involvement in review will be evident through the monitoring and evaluation systems that enable teams and ultimately the whole organisation to evidence change affected by participation.

Organisational systems and culture

When Professor Eileen Munro was asked by the British Government to undertake a review of child protection in 2010, she used systems theory to examine the prevailing conditions and concluded that there had been too much prescription such as national performance indicators, targets and local bureaucracy resulting in an over-proceduralised system. Munro (2011: 6) suggested that 'forces have come together to create a defensive system that puts so much emphasis on procedures and recording that insufficient attention is given to developing and supporting the expertise to work effectively with children, young people and families.'

In her final report, Munro devoted a chapter to the organisational context, where she explores to what extent it is supporting effective social work practice. A strong message of her report, which has been generally accepted as applicable also to adult services and community care, is the development of a learning culture at macro, meso and micro levels with an expectation that organisations should be better at monitoring, learning and adjusting their practice.

This contributes to achieving the goal of becoming a 'learning organisation', creating a culture that allows individuals and teams to develop their knowledge and skills and share them with others in the organisation, thus becoming a 'community of practice'. Learning organisations assume that all their members are competent and individuals and teams can perform to the maximum of their capabilities with minimum supervision. Senge (1990: 3) defined a learning organisation as one 'where people continually expand their capacity to create the results they truly desire, where new and expansive patterns of thinking are nurtured, where collective aspiration is set free, and where people are continually learning how to learn together.'

> **Reflection**
> - To what extent is your work agency a 'learning organisation'?
> - Does your experience of participating in a team mirror the suggestions above?
> - What can you do personally and within your team to contribute to the development of a 'community of practice'?

One of Munro's recommendations is that when carrying out serious case reviews (SCRs) after a death or serious injury to a child, Local Safeguarding Children

Boards (LSCBs) should not focus on mistakes and blame but use systems methodology to explain why things happened, to learn from practice and disseminate this learning. She proposes making the reviews more independent, not evaluated by Ofsted. A review team should be selected reflecting the range of professionals involved in the case being reviewed. This will challenge views on accountability, making SCRs a means of learning from experience rather than focusing on determining liability.

The Munro proposals advocate teams working differently, basing their practice on evidence and being more child and family focused. Individual social workers that had arguably become de-skilled by bureaucracy and managerialism might now be expected to work in a more creative and autonomous way making professional judgements. For such collaborative working and to develop your own knowledge and skills, you will need emotional intelligence and resilience as discussed in Chapter 4.

Although it was a review of child protection, many of the Munro recommendations and proposals for culture change, as stated above, apply to and are being considered by adult social services and community care.

Case example

In April 2006, the London Borough of Hackney Children's Social Care embarked on a change of culture, launched significantly as 'The Way We Want to Do Things Here'. Through a consultation period with staff and partners and taking into account national developments, by November 2007 a change programme was published with the 'brand' name 'Reclaiming Social Work', described as a whole systems approach to child and family social work. An expectation is that in addition to social work skills and a sound knowledge base, practitioners need to be confident, articulate, professional and have stamina and determination.

The reorganisation of services included former teams becoming multidisciplinary Social Work Units (SWU) with a good deal of autonomy, joint working and sharing of information. Units headed by a Consultant Social Worker have a unit coordinator who provides administrative support for tasks previously undertaken by social workers. Each child and family is known to each SWU member. The SWU meets weekly to agree tasks that need to be undertaken that week. Resources include a children's practitioner and clinician time.

Reflection

- If you were freed from too many prescriptions, performance indicators and targets, how would you be accountable?
- What might be the mindset and mix of skills you need for effective teamwork, including the use of intuition and creativity?

Responsibility, accountability and liability

An element of the Contexts and Organisations PDF domain (The College of Social Work, 2012) is 'Knowing your role and responsibilities'. As a social worker, you have a responsibility to follow statutory duties and powers, but you also have a responsibility to learn and develop, to share your learning with your team and, working with the team, to share learning within your organisation. A criticism of social work in recent years is that it has become too risk averse, with a blame culture focusing on determining where liability lay when there have been tragedies and errors made. Possible culture changes have been suggested earlier in this chapter, although as a social worker you remain accountable and answerable to others for your behaviour and professional judgements.

You are accountable to your employer and to the ethics of your profession. As a team member you are also accountable and answerable to your team. A challenge from explorations in this chapter is for you to consider a model of responsibility that involves you and your team owning the ability and power to develop, be resourceful and creative, and to acknowledge personal responsibility when things go well and when mistakes occur.

Organisational frameworks

Organisations can have a variety of more or less complex management structures that are traditionally depicted in pyramid shape organisational charts, with the director or chief executive officer (CEO) at the top and lines of management indicating relationships and the location of teams 'down' the hierarchy. The 'link pin' structure discussed earlier in the chapter relates to such an organisational framework. The conventional depiction of an organisational chart can be challenged, as it suggests that more senior positions in an organisation are 'higher' and can institutionalise the supremacy of senior management and power relationships.

There are inverted organisational charts that defy the traditional pyramid structure, placing work teams at the top, going down to middle managers and operational teams, with the director or CEO being at the bottom of the structure, suggesting they are supporting the work of the organisation. Whether this is the experience of practitioners or merely a pictorial device depends on the organisational culture and the actual behaviour of the variety of post holders throughout the organisational framework.

Whichever way they are envisaged, the links in an organisational chart represent lines of communication and accountability that you need to understand, get to know and work within to show capability in the Contexts and Organisations PCF domain outlined at the beginning of this chapter. Who each person in an organisation 'reports to' is not always completely clear and may change with reorganisations. An exercise that can prove enlightening is to ask members in a team to draw an organisational chart of the whole organisation, or a portion of it including the team's accountability, and compare the individual versions. It rarely results in a uniform perception of the organisational structure and can clarify team members' understanding as differences are discussed and adjusted.

Case example: Two integrated social care teams

A relatively small unitary authority organised adult services and community care in geographical, health and social care integrated teams located in Healthy Living Centres. Two geographically adjacent teams, composed in each case of approximately ten social care and twenty health staff, were headed by two team managers, one with a social work qualification, the other a health professional. The management in one team of some ten social care staff by a health professional, and in the other team of twenty health staff by a social work professional was found not to be completely satisfactory.

As a result of staff changes and budgetary revision, a new arrangement was instituted where the two teams remained integrated but one social work qualified 'floating' manager became responsible for the management of the social care workers in both teams and one health professional similarly managed the health staff in both teams. Each of these two new managers was based in one of the geographical locations but regularly visited the other location for individual and group meetings. The two managers had to work closely together because, although they had separate sets of responsibilities, there was a good deal of overlap in their involvement with both teams.

Under both arrangements, supervision of social care staff was undertaken by team-based social work qualified senior practitioners and of health staff by team coordinators for district nurses. The team mangers were 'link pins', as they also attended meetings of operational teams; the integrated teams were 'matrix structures' comprising a variety of social care and health professionals; each team had boundaried social care and health spheres of influence and other communication and shared interest subgroups that could be recognised as 'systems approaches'; both teams used 'network approaches' to liaise with and connect with other professionals within the Healthy Living Centres and further afield.

Supervision

The need for social workers to receive regular supervision is generally accepted as essential to provide three interrelated functions that Kadushin and Harkness (2002) suggest are administrative, educational and supportive. Thus supervision should enable you to balance elements of:

- being accountable to the team and organisation's management for work undertaken;
- an opportunity for reflection and learning;
- receiving support as an individual.

Inquiries into tragedies such as Lord Laming's report into the death of Victoria Climbié (Laming, 2003) have criticised senior managers accountable for the practice in their departments and team managers and senior social workers for providing inadequate supervision, as well as individual social workers for negligence in their work.

The traditional expectation is that a team leader or senior practitioner will provide individual one-to-one supervision to social workers but, in line with this textbook's focus on teamworking skills, the extent to which a team can have a role in providing the functions outlined above is worthy of note. Tsui (2005: 23) states:

> In human service organisations, supervision models often reflect the level of control exercised by the agency . . . At one extreme is the casework model, which is based on a high level of administrative accountability. At the other extreme is the autonomous practice model where there is a high degree of professional autonomy . . . Between these extremes are the group supervision model . . . the peer supervision model . . . and the team service delivery model.

Accountability for a social worker's standard of practice is a line management responsibility and we noted above that as a social worker you are accountable to your employer and to the profession. However, being accountable and answerable to your team could be seen as part of line management accountability dovetailing with the team's role in allocation, planning, delegating and coordination of work.

The educational and supportive functions lend themselves to more substantial possibilities for team supervision. A team can provide a considerable level of teaching and learning opportunities as well as mutual support. In group supervision, it is usual for a social worker to present a case focusing on critical issues and dilemmas. The designated supervisor facilitates the group, enabling team members to explore and analyse the material, drawing on their knowledge and experience, exchanging viewpoints and providing new insights. Tsui (2005: 24) suggests that group supervision can include the tasks of 'providing emotional support, providing practical consultation, team building, and addressing agency issues'.

A related model with origins in family therapy consultation is for a social worker to present a case uninterrupted, concluding with a concern or dilemma and then allow the rest of the team to discuss possibilities and suggest hypotheses without participation from the social worker who presented. This allows the team to explore issues without the worker feeling they have to explain their position or defend their viewpoint. The presenter in due course responds to the team and there is further discussion with everyone participating, but it is up to the worker what insights and suggestions they take away to apply in practice.

In original versions of this model, the worker left the room after the presentation to allow team discussion to take place, returned to hear the feedback and respond to the team, and then left again to allow for further team discussion on the responses in a repeat of the process. Thus the model can be adapted to the extent of independent consultation thought appropriate.

Peer supervision is not unlike the first group supervision model described above but it does not rely on a designated supervisor. Team members, whether the whole team or an appropriate sub-group (or sphere of shared interest), participate equally and with sensitivity in an atmosphere of mutual help and sharing. This suits a close-knit, cohesive and non-hierarchical team or group. It requires discipline, as no individual chairs the interaction. The team member presenting a case can be allowed some control of the discussion.

A service delivery model is typically used in multidisciplinary teams working to a transdisciplinary or metadisciplinary approach, based on the premise that one practitioner can perform the role of other team members by working with a service user under the supervision of individuals from the other disciplines in the team. A whole team interdisciplinary approach is usually used for initial assessment and planning, but only one or two team members implement the plan, provide the services and arrange supervision. Regardless of who is engaging in intervention with a service user, practitioners are still accountable for areas related to their individual discipline and for training and supervising the team member who is delivering the service.

It can be seen from the examples above that a team focus in supervision can provide opportunities for team members' reflection and learning and to receive the support of peers and of the team as a whole. In addition to enhancing practitioners' professional development, these supervision models can contribute to a learning team and organisation and to the growth of a community of practice.

Chapter summary

Moving on from the foundations laid in previous chapters, this chapter set out to apply aspects of teamworking outlined earlier to practice working within organisations. It explored the capabilities within the PCF domain of Contexts and Organisations, as they relate to teamworking, of social workers getting to know their organisation and influencing it, and seeing teams as a vehicle for this.

We considered four approaches to conceptualise the structure of teamwork within organisations: 'link pin structure', 'matrix structures', 'systems approaches' and 'network approaches'. These highlighted channels of communication and formal and informal networks that social workers can use to engage with the organisation. This led to discussion of the importance of organisational and team culture. Service user and carer participation was explored using a whole systems approach, highlighting the need for organisations to develop a culture, structure, effective practice and review systems that evidence the full involvement of people who use their services and carers.

The chapter referred to the Munro review of child protection using systems theory to conclude that prescription and bureaucratic procedures had tended to de-skill social workers. Munro promotes a learning rather than a blame culture and social workers working in new ways, including the use of intuition and creativity and making professional judgements, leading to the development of 'communities of practice'. These considerations led to reflection on responsibility, accountability and liability, and the challenge to consider a model of responsibility that involves you and your team owning the ability and power to develop, be resourceful, creative and to acknowledge personal responsibility when things go well and when mistakes occur.

As part of working in organisations, we considered the complexity of organisational frameworks as depicted by organisational charts and the need to understand lines of communication and accountability to the team. Finally, the chapter outlined the three functions of professional supervision as administrative accountability, educational or enabling learning, and being supportive. Discussion included a reminder that a social worker can be accountable to the team, in addition to their employer and to the profession, and that teams can contribute to the educational and supportive functions of supervision through group and peer supervision and a service delivery model.

The overarching themes in this chapter include:

- The need for social workers to be accountable to their employers, to the profession, to service users and carers and to their team.
- The challenge of developing learning organisations and communities of practice and how teams can contribute to this.
- The insights provided by a whole systems approach to consideration of working in organisations, such as systems approaches to teams in organisations, service user and carer participation, the organisational culture as highlighted by the conclusions of the Munro review, the 'Reclaiming Social Work' programme in the London Borough of Hackney, and the benefit of understanding teams and teamworking within wider meso and macro systemic contexts.

Further reading

Belbin, R.M. (2000) *Beyond the Team*. Oxford: Butterworth-Heinemann. In addition to providing further insights into Belbin's long established work on teams and Team Role theory, this book explores the balance between teamwork and professional roles. It introduces a colour-coded system to understand top-down and bottom-up communication and feedback in the workplace.

Hafford-Letchfield, T. (2009) *Management and Organisations in Social Work*, 2nd edn. Exeter: Learning Matters. This textbook takes a broad look at influences on social work management in organisations. It explores structures and cultures, service user involvement and learning organisations.

Hughes, M. and Wearing, M. (2007) *Organisations and Management in Social Work*. London: Sage. A theoretical and value-based consideration of social work in organisations, including accountability and participation and how organisations are experienced by workers.

7 Multidisciplinary teams

Introduction

In this chapter, we will consider teamworking applied to teams that bring together a number of practitioners form different professional disciplines and are located in one work base. Following an outline of a number of features relating to multidisciplinary teams, exploring factors that help and hinder effective work in them, the chapter will review skills needed to work effectively in such teams.

The next chapter will address the teamworking aspects of inter-professional collaboration – professionals from various agencies that collaborate and work in partnership to help a common service user but not necessarily as part of an identifiable permanent team in one location.

The need for social workers to collaborate with other professionals has received much attention in recent years but is not something new. Social workers have always liaised and worked in partnership with a variety of professionals. However, the past twenty-five years or so have seen moves towards partnership in professional education and the increasing integration of practitioners from different professional disciplines in work teams. The Centre for the Advancement of Interprofessional Education (CAIPE), for instance, was set up in 1987 and promotes the improvement of collaborative practice through social care, health care and social work professionals learning and working together.

In the field of mental health, Primary Care Liaison Teams emerged around the same time that CAIPE was formed, as a result of the trend for care in the community rather than in large psychiatric hospitals, and developed into multidisciplinary Community Mental Health Teams (CMHTs) as we know them today. They typically consist of consultant psychiatrists, community psychiatric nurses, occupational therapists, social workers, family workers, care managers and other professionals such as clinical psychologists.

Another example of multidisciplinary work is found in Youth Offending Teams (YOTs), set up following the 1998 Crime and Disorder Act. They may comprise professionals from social work, the police service, probation service, health, education, Connexions, youth work, housing and psychology. Functional roles can include workers with responsibility for bail and remand, young offender panel, resettlement, parenting support, reparation, prevention, Triage (low risk) work, intensive support (high risk) monitoring and the coordination of volunteers. As suggested by this list, the size of the team can be 25–30 practitioners.

In schools, teachers are increasingly part of multidisciplinary teams working with classroom assistants, social workers, family care workers, nursery nurses, educational psychologists, other related workers and parent volunteers.

Terminology and concepts

Terms such as multi-professional care, multidisciplinary, interdisciplinary and multi-agency work, and inter-agency collaboration are used in various settings, so it is worth exploring some implications. Based on their review of literature about multidisciplinary teamworking in education, Wilson and Pirrie (2000: 3) suggest that 'the distinction between "inter" and "multi" is based upon three dimensions. These are: numerical; territorial; and epistemological'.

Numerically, the terms inter-professional or interdisciplinary work could apply to just two professional disciplines cooperating as they work together. The term 'multi', and multidisciplinary teamwork in particular, suggests several disciplines working together as a team.

Territorial issues arise from the impact of professional boundaries in multidisciplinary teamwork. In earlier research, Pirrie et al. (1998) quote a focus group participant as saying 'interdisciplinary . . . it's like you are crossing into another space'. When individuals come together from different professional disciplines with differing characteristics such as training, traditional ways of working, cultures, jargon, ethos, values and pay expectations, working effectively as a team can be particularly difficult. Daley (1989: 116) used the idea of 'organisational tribalism', suggesting 'tribal allegiances' are 'the product of unfounded and stereotypical assumptions'. Stereotyping is an issue that we will pursue further below.

An epistemological dimension, or an understanding of the essential nature of inter-disciplinary teamworking itself, takes us beyond the contribution of each professional discipline to a potentially new way of working. This might be conceptualised as a metadiscipline within which there are disciplinary strands. We have already noted in previous chapters that the interdependence of a variety of team and functional roles is a positive aspect that can lead to synergy. Writing about health care, Nolan (1995: 306) suggests 'interdisciplinary care although not denying the importance of specific skills, seeks to blur the professional boundaries and requires trust, tolerance and a willingness to share responsibility'.

Melin Emilsson (2011) conducted research into ways of working by a multi-professional older people's team in England. To analyse teamwork, she uses a model originally proposed by Thylefors et al. (2005) outlining three processes:

1. *Multi-professional* – a collaborative process within which members of different disciplines work with service users independently, retaining specialisms but sharing information.

2. *Inter-professional* – a deeper level of collaboration with more joint work and professionals from different disciplines pooling their knowledge.
3. *Trans-professional* – an integrative work process where disciplinary boundaries are blurred. Team members and their tasks are interdependent.

Melin Emilsson (2011) found complementary, non-competitive roles among different disciplines, with social work having an impact on health care for older people. However, she refers to what she studied as 'collaborative cross-professional teamwork', since it did not fit exactly with any of the processes described above. She nevertheless suggests we should not be unduly pessimistic about the role of social work in multidisciplinary teams.

These studies to some extent are engaged in clarifying semantics. The 'metadiscipline' approach of Wilson and Pirrie (2000) seems congruent with Thylefors and colleagues' (2005) 'trans-professional' teamwork.

Professional role boundaries

We have previously explored the idea that teams can be analysed systemically and be seen to work as a close knit, cohesive family or a dysfunctional one. Government initiatives and legislation at macro level can threaten professional role boundaries at the micro level of multidisciplinary teamworking. The Mental Health Act (MHA) 2007, for instance, replaced approved social workers (ASWs) with approved mental health professionals (AMHPs). The previous requirement of the 1983 MHA for an ASW with additional post-qualifying training to interview patients and recommend compulsory hospital detention jointly with two doctors under a section of the Act – 'sectioning' – now applies to AMHPs, a role that can include nurses, psychologists and occupational therapists, as well as social workers, thus emphasising a multidisciplinary approach but blurring the boundaries of social workers' responsibilities. The 2007 MHA also replaced the role of a responsible medical officer (RMO), entitled to make the decision about continuation of compulsion after a patient is detained under an order, with a responsible clinician (RC) that could be a nurse, psychologist, occupational therapist or social worker, as well as a doctor, thus blurring the health and social work, doctor and nursing boundaries.

Based on participant research into CMHTs, Bailey and Liyanage (2012) see the role of the mental health social worker as a 'political pawn' within government pressures for change to reconfigure health and social care. Through their research they found that mental health social workers experienced conflict between a unique social work contribution and their multidisciplinary role as generic care coordinators. Another finding was that mental health social workers experienced stigma and reduced status in a service dominated by health.

Multidisciplinary teamwork makes considerable demands on you as a social worker, and on other professionals for that matter. On the one hand, it is important that you are clear about your specific contribution as a social worker to a multidisciplinary team. The British Association of Social Workers (BASW, 2010) policy on social work in multidisciplinary mental health teams, for instance, seeks to clarify the role of social workers. It states that 'The mental health development group of BASW has endorsed the following definition: "Working with users and carers, social workers promote a unique holistic, recovery orientated, value based, social care/social inclusion model." NIMHE (April 2006)'.

However, a contrasting view is that multidisciplinary synergy is attained through a positive blurring of disciplinary boundaries or merging of professional roles resulting in new ways of working. A balancing act would seems to be required of you with the need to make a contribution to the team from your particular professional tradition, but your contribution also having to be interdependent, complementary and collaborative with that of other professional disciplines all working towards a common goal.

Case example: Two integrated social care teams

The changes in team management for the two integrated social care teams outlined in the case example in Chapter 6 question to what extent each team is fully integrated. Social care and health professionals belong to one geographical team but different team managers from social care and from health manage them. They have no joint funding, thus the costs of services have to be allocated to one budget or the other. Their computer systems are not compatible, so social care practitioners cannot access electronic health records and vice versa. The social care team manager and a social care administrator have been granted access to health computer records, while the team manager for health staff and a health administrator have access to social care records. Each service user and patient has separate social care and health files with hard copy paper records. These have been filed together side by side so that practitioners from either discipline can easily look through them both.

The traditional ways of working of the two disciplines are different. Health staff are used to quick visits to check on a patient's health and medication. A district nurse stated in a record entry that the patient was 'not compliant' and she would not be visiting again because of this. Social care staff tend to pay more attention to wider social and emotional aspects of a service user's circumstances, would attempt to understand why a service user may not be taking medicine and use social work skills to explain the importance of medication.

There are those who wonder whether social care and health staff are 'co-located' in one team, rather than truly integrated. However, on balance there is a feeling that better communication and collaboration are possible under the present arrangements and that service users/patients receive a better service than they would if the two disciplines had separate teams.

Role adequacy and legitimacy

Loughran et al. (2010) researched the reluctance of social workers to address substance misuse problems with service users. They explored factors that increased 'role adequacy' (feeling knowledgeable about one's work) and 'role legitimacy' (believing that one has the right to address certain service user issues). These two interrelated theoretical constructs are of significance for social workers in multidisciplinary teams.

If as a social worker you are seconded into or you transfer to work in a setting with a specific service user group (mental health, youth justice, education), you may feel threatened and excluded because you are not familiar with that discipline and culture. This may affect your role adequacy and legitimacy. The team leader or manager may be someone from another professional discipline, not social work qualified, so as a social worker you may feel misunderstood and unsupported rather than your role being confirmed and enhanced.

Your role adequacy can be enhanced if your work is grounded in professional social work values, by being capable in your use of teamworking skills, pursuing continuous professional development, regularly updating your social work knowledge and being guided by research. In addition, you will need an adequate and appropriate knowledge of the service user group your multidisciplinary team works with. As a member of a CMHT, for instance, you may use a psycho-social approach to assess a person's needs and how social issues impact on the mental health of the service user. However:

> Having said that, as a social worker practising in this area you would be working with other professionals, and service users, who do know the diagnostic criteria and categories well. You will, therefore, need to have some understanding and a degree of proficiency about psychiatric definitions and treatments.
>
> (Martin, 2010:124)

Your role legitimacy is the extent to which you believe that working with a particular service user, or group of service users, is your responsibility. Role legitimacy will include the belief that you have the right to ask a mental health service user or an older person, for instance, about their medication and for any information that is relevant to their psychiatric or medical condition. Whether you feel that your service users believe you have the right to ask them such questions will also influence your role legitimacy. Some of the factors that enhance your role adequacy, particularly those concerning knowledge and experience relating to specific service user groups, will also boost your role legitimacy.

Case example

In a Youth Offending Team (YOT) that includes a variety of professionals, as suggested towards the beginning of this chapter, practitioners refer to themselves as 'a YOT worker', although they may be a social work, probation, police, education, health professional or a support worker without a professional qualification. While bringing to the team a skill set and underpinning knowledge from their disciplines, within the YOT ethos and culture they see themselves as belonging to an integrated multidisciplinary team.

One health professional is very organised, dependable and pays great attention to detail. Other team members jokingly call her 'matron'. Her skills and professionalism are easily transferable to a criminal Court setting, where the judiciary have a great respect for her and value her contributions and interventions. A number of the young offenders and their families have had negative experiences with social workers in the past, are very critical of social work and are resistant to engage with social workers. The team members with a social work qualification do not feel threatened by this but have experienced that by being regarded as 'YOT workers', young people and their families accept their involvement more readily.

The case example above may suggest that YOT appears to approximate the concept of a metadiscipline within which there are disciplinary strands.

Stereotyping

We live in a complex world where our senses are bombarded by information. One way of coping with this is to categorise our understanding, including how we perceive other people. Stereotypes can be seen as personal and social constructs or simplified pictures in our minds of people and events in the world. The American journalist Walter Lippmann first used the term 'stereotype' in the psychological sense as we understand it today in 1922, suggesting our actions are not based on a direct knowledge of the 'real' world because the 'real environment is altogether too big, too complex and too fleeting for direct acquaintance' (Lippmann, 1922: 16). We categorise people, including colleague team members, by gender, age, appearance, nationality, ethnicity, accent, attire, job title and professional discipline. Multidisciplinary teams can be large and multifaceted, thus require some sorting within our minds for us to understand them.

In stereotyping, a group of people are identified by one or more particular characteristics. We then tend to attribute a set of additional (stereotypical) characteristics to the group as a whole. When we identify a person as having the meaningful characteristic, job title or professional discipline, we also attribute the stereotypical characteristic to them – for example, police officers are aggressive, medical consultants are arrogant, and nurses are caring.

While simplifying and categorising the social world can be helpful, stereotyping mostly involves inaccurate judgements. The contents of many stereotypes are often derogatory (e.g. aggressive, arrogant, lazy, unintelligent) and stereotyping can be linked to prejudice against a group. Like caricatures, stereotypes exaggerate the characteristics of a person or group.

Activity

List the characteristics of one or more of the roles below. Jot these down quickly as they come to your mind without stopping to think too deeply about them.

Try to undertake this activity with colleague professionals within your work team, fellow students, or even with friends and relatives. It will be interesting to compare notes and you may find some common stereotypes emerging.

- Police officer
- General practitioner
- Psychologist
- Psychiatrist
- Nurse
- Teacher
- Social worker

Stereotypes can be processed quickly and efficiently, so we use them when under pressure of time or information overload. Reviewing your lists of characteristics for some of the roles above, did you engage in faulty thinking or inaccurate judgements?

We may not view others stereotypically if we pay attention to information that is inconsistent with the stereotype, such as knowing calm, quiet police officers, noting that some medical consultants can be modest and unassuming, and some nurses cold and indifferent. Stereotyping is not just an individual process; we categorise groups, such as professional disciplines, and the categorisation process can lead to accentuation of differences between groups ('them and us') and similarities and favouritism within a group ('one of us'). You usually focus on the professional group to which you see yourself as belonging (your in-group) and judge yourself as different from individuals in professional groups that you do not see yourself as being part of (out-groups).

Reflection

In your experience, how do social workers regard and get on with police officers, doctors, health visitors, solicitors, teachers, and so on? Does your personal position about this fit in with or differ from possible stereotypes?

Thus it is important for you as a social worker within a multidisciplinary team that you establish and retain your identity based on your training, values and professional ethos. The stereotype that the general public or other professionals may have of social workers might include characteristics such as lentil-eating, sandal-wearing, left wing, *Guardian* reader, meddling, overbearing and incompetent do-gooder!

Language and culture

People tend to employ stereotypes to support their prejudices and be critical of others, not the other way around. The variety of descriptions that we use about others can sometimes include apparent contradictions. Edwards (1996) points out that an analysis of political, professional or personal discourse can reveal the function of language and ideological positions that exist within it. In the same way that we use gender stereotypes such as engaging in 'women talk' and 'male conversations', the use of dialects and accents within language and certain words and topics relate to class and socio-economic level. Certain professionals traditionally tend to come from particular socio-economic backgrounds. Professions have jargon that other disciplines find difficult to understand. Our professional discourse can reveal our individual views and values.

Stereotypes can be viewed as social representations and reflect the professional culture of the group, communicated between its members, thus making us more comfortable within that group. Different professional cultures will differ in the social representations they hold and in the explanations contained within them. A 'cultural model' is 'a cognitive schema that is intersubjectively shared by a social group' (D'Andrade, 1990: 99). Cultural stereotypes apply to wider social groups as well as to organisational and professional cultures.

Power dynamics and inclusion

We noted in previous chapters that the power dynamics and emotional aspects of a number of individual human beings working together could affect the effectiveness of a team. There are hierarchies within some disciplines – medical consultants tend to have a higher status than nurses, the police service has ranks. So there may be power dynamics and competition for control that affect you as a social worker. There is a danger that you might feel intimidated by professionals from longer established disciplines with a higher status or longer training than you have.

Similarly, there is a danger that team members without a professional qualification may feel marginalised. Social and health care assistants and administrative staff are a part of the team. Their contribution is different but valid. Teamworking implies including them in information dissemination, formal communications and in contributing to making decisions.

Decision-making

The way decisions are taken is important. Multidisciplinary team members need to communicate openly about their priorities, professional judgements, possible prejudices and loyalties. In action research with multidisciplinary teams in the UK, Øvretveit (1995) came to the conclusion that:

- effective decision-making is central to successful multidisciplinary teamwork;
- improvements come from paying attention to both formal and informal features of team organisation;
- suitable formal decision-making procedures are necessary for teams to survive.

Informal features of team organisation include traditional power bases and 'games', status positions, emotional allegiances, belief and influence sub-systems, and unofficial communication channels. Formal features include team meetings, agreed ways of making decisions, allocating work and ways of dealing with service users' requests and involvement.

Service user participation

A service user can be considered a member of a multidisciplinary team. Arguably, someone who has a diverse team of different professionals discussing their welfare should be entitled to the chance to contribute. Listening to service users and working in partnership with them is in keeping with social work values and something social workers can contribute to multidisciplinary teams. The ability of different service users to participate should be taken into account. Service users able to articulate their needs strongly may more easily influence decisions and might make some professionals feel threatened. The relationship with easy-going service users should not be different from that with demanding ones.

It may be that some carers and people who use services need help, support or training to develop ways in which they can participate at team level. One way is to form a service user partnership or reference group to regularly discuss ways in which they can participate, remembering that formal meetings may not be the preferred or most comfortable way of contributing for some service users.

Skills needed in multidisciplinary work

The rest of this chapter will review skills needed in multidisciplinary teamworking. A skill, the capacity to undertake a task successfully and proficiently, can be learnt and developed but, as previously stated, is difficult to isolate from actions that need to be taken by professionals, the qualities of the professional as a person and the underpinning professional values that influence how skills are used. Skills will therefore be explored in this wider context. Those outlined are not exclusive to working in multidisciplinary teams but they are reviewed here with that focus. It is helpful to explore them in categories, although these overlap. The categories involve the skills needed for:

- Self-management
- Professionalism
- Interaction and collaboration with team colleagues
- Networking

Self-management

Self-awareness is a starting point in managing yourself as a member of a multidisciplinary team. In addition to following your job description, in joining the team you will have formally or informally met the requirements of a person specification. Can you readily outline what these are? Are you fulfilling and developing them? Be aware of the informal roles you play in the team – thinker, doer, carer, leader, achiever, etc. Do you have a tendency to play any negative roles – complainer, critic, blamer, detractor, and so on? Aim for self-congruence, being comfortable with the person you are. This will increase your self-confidence.

Organise and manage your time. Assertiveness skills will help you discuss with others in an Adult-to-Adult way, and if necessary question, the nature and number of tasks that you are asked to undertake. Maintain a life/work balance to manage stress. Set yourself personal goals. This self-leadership will help you develop both as a person and professionally. Monitor your emotions and those of others in the team so that you can understand the emotions of others and manage your own.

Professionalism

Take responsibility for your conduct, practice and learning. Explore your social work role within the multidisciplinary team. Reflect on the social work contribution you make to the team and the social work skills you use but do not see this as an isolated or exclusive position. Confirm and enhance your role, thus strengthening it rather than feeling the stigma of perceived reduced status compared with other professionals. Develop confidence in your own professional status through your continuous professional development.

In formal and informal ways, learn about the service user group with which you are working and the background, culture and language of the professionals with whom you work. Develop your role adequacy through increased knowledge. Contribute to team development by sharing your professional ethos and learning with others. This will develop your role legitimacy and the confidence in your perceived right to address issues relating to the team's service user group.

Be reliable, delivering as agreed when you take on responsibilities. Be accountable for your work. Develop your written communication skills, paying attention to the standard of your records and reports and being professional in your letters and email communication. Critically reflect on and analyse your involvement with service users and the decisions you take. Follow the guidance of the Critical Reflection and Analysis PCF domain:

> Show creativity in tackling and solving problems, by considering a range of options to solve dilemmas. Use reflective practice techniques to evaluate and critically analyse information, gained from a variety of sources, to construct and test hypotheses and make explicit evidence-informed decisions.
>
> (The College of Social Work, 2012)

Seek supervision from the person nominated to provide it for you. The Social Work Reform Board (SWRB, 2010) recommended that employers should:

> Make sure that supervision takes place at least weekly for the first six weeks of employment of a newly qualified social worker, at least fortnightly for the duration of the first six months, and a minimum of monthly supervision thereafter. Ensure that supervision sessions last at least an hour and a half of uninterrupted time.

In a multidisciplinary team, your supervisor may be from another professional discipline but you should regard this person as a consultant and coach, rather than expecting that you should be in the role of apprentice to an experienced qualified social worker.

Interaction and collaboration with team colleagues

As a team player, develop your interpersonal communication skills and relationships with all team members. Listen to other team members with empathetic understanding and pay attention to verbal and non-verbal messages. Be aware of power dynamics and emotionally charged issues. Aim to be open and straightforward, disclosing your views and position, not playing games. Do not feel threatened or excluded and work so that others should not feel so either. Avoid cliques and exclusive sub-groups.

See yourself as fitting in with others in the team in an interdependent way. Be flexible and willing to cooperate. Accept that others may have different ways of acting and behaving, and that you have to accommodate others' views. Attend team meetings regularly and participate fully in them. Follow and contribute to agreed team processes for allocating work and ways of engaging with service users. Explore differences of opinion and be willing to compromise. Take a problem-solving approach to manage any conflict and making decisions. Contribute to clarifying the purpose, aims and objectives of the team.

Conceptualise teamworking as participative, involving all team members whatever their perceived status. Challenge your stereotypical thinking. Work with service users and empower them to be involved and participate in as many aspects of the life of the team as possible.

Networking

Get to know your organisation, key personnel and channels of communication. Aim to contribute to your organisation by finding ways to influence policies and procedures rather than taking a negative, critical approach. Follow the guidance of the Contexts and Organisations PCF domain:

> Take account of legal, operational and policy contexts, proactively engage with your own organisation and contribute to its evaluation and development. Proactively engage with colleagues, and a range of organisations to identify, assess, plan and support the needs of service users and communities.
>
> (The College of Social Work, 2012)

Develop contacts with like-minded individuals in other professions and teams, getting to know them and finding common ground. Build networks of support and opportunities to share knowledge and information. Attend appropriate events, meetings and conferences where you can mix with and exchange views with other professionals. Use on-line professional networks to complement face-to-face contact.

Chapter summary

This chapter has explored teamworking within multidisciplinary teams. It acknowledged the trends towards multi-professional partnerships with examples such as CMHTs, YOTs and education. We noted the varied terminology used, accepting that distinctions are based on three dimensions: numerical, territorial and epistemological. Numerically, the terms inter-professional and interdisciplinary can apply to just two disciplines, whereas multidisciplinary suggests several disciplines working together. Territorial issues corresponded with the ideas that different disciplines have 'tribal allegiances' due to their different characteristics. An epistemological dimension took us beyond the contribution of each professional discipline to consider new ways of working that might be regarded as a metadiscipline with disciplinary strands or trans-professional teamwork.

This led to exploration of professional role boundaries and considering whether their blurring emphasises a multidisciplinary approach or results in a conflict of roles and threat to social work. The chapter emphasised a positive view of the role of social work in multidisciplinary work through enhancement of 'role adequacy' (feeling knowledgeable about one's work) and 'role legitimacy' (believing that one has the right to address certain service user issues), which included the need to have an adequate knowledge of the service user group you are working with.

We further examined how professionals from different disciplines may regard each other through a discussion of stereotyping, professional language and culture, and power dynamics and inclusion. We noted research conclusions suggesting that effective decision-making is central to successful multidisciplinary teamwork; that improvements come from paying attention to both formal and informal features of team organisation; and that suitable formal decision-making procedures are necessary for teams to survive. We acknowledged the importance of involving service users in decisions and the possibility of regarding service users and carers as members of a multidisciplinary team.

The rest of the chapter outlined skills needed in multidisciplinary work under the categories of self-management, professionalism, interaction and collaboration with team colleagues, and networking.

Further reading

Onyett, S. (2003) *Teamworking in Mental Health*. Basingstoke: Palgave Macmillan. Although specific to mental health and focusing on CMHTs, this textbook explores aspects of multidisciplinary teams and teamworking that are applicable to other settings.

Payne, M. (2000) *Teamwork in Multiprofessional Care*. Basingstoke: Palgrave Macmillan. Although now a few years old, this remains one of the few textbooks to address teamwork from a health and care (including social work) perspective. It explores the multidisciplinary nature of some teams and the need to network with other agencies.

8 Inter-professional collaboration

Introduction

Taking the ideas from the previous chapter further, this one will explore aspects of inter-agency collaboration and partnership by professionals from a variety of organisations working with a common service user but not necessarily based in the same work location. It will review some of the barriers and obstacles to collaboration before moving on to outline skills needed and actions that can be taken by professionals to overcome difficulties, qualities of a practitioner and underpinning professional values in inter-professional and multi-agency collaboration.

Lack of collaboration

Inquiries into tragedies such as the death of Jonathan Zito, killed by mental health patient Christopher Clunis (Ritchie et al., 1994), and Victoria Climbié (Laming, 2003) have consistently criticised the agencies and professionals involved, in particular highlighting:

- unclear responsibilities and accountability;
- poor communication;
- inadequate planning and coordination of services;
- lack of collaboration and information sharing between agencies.

Jonathan Zito was the victim of an unprovoked stabbing in December 1992 by Christopher Clunis, who had been diagnosed with paranoid schizophrenia and was receiving community care and supervision by psychiatric and social services at the time. Over a period of five and a half years he had contact with psychiatrists, social workers, the police, community psychiatric nurses, the Courts, probation service, hostel staff and private sector care workers. He had been admitted to psychiatric hospitals, remanded in prison and police custody, lived in a bail hostel, two rehabilitation hostels, two hostels for homeless people and a number of bed and breakfast accommodation addresses. However, it appears there was no supportive 'team' around him.

Eight-year-old Victoria Climbié was killed in February 2000, ten months after arriving in England from the Ivory Coast, by her great-aunt and partner following abuse, torture and many injuries. Local authority social services departments, hospitals, the police, the National Society for the Prevention of Cruelty to Children (NSPCC) and local churches had contact with Victoria. Nonetheless, no one agency had the full picture of what was happening. Lord Laming, who conducted the inquiry into Victoria's death, was also asked to prepare a report on safeguarding arrangements following the death of 17-month-old Peter Connolly (known at the time of his death as Baby P) in August 2008. Peter was on the child protection register of Haringey Council that had been criticised for Victoria's death eight years previously.

Some thirty years before the deaths of Victoria and Peter, a public enquiry into the death of Maria Colwell outlined criticisms very similar to those listed above. Seven-year-old Maria was killed by her stepfather in 1973 after she had been fostered but returned to live with her biological mother and new partner. Neighbours and teachers voiced concerns to various agencies that did not coordinate the information and work together to safeguard Maria. Tragically, it seems that lessons have not been learned concerning the dangers of inadequate inter-professional collaboration.

These examples, among many others, highlight the crucial need for professionals and agencies to coordinate their contributions when working with vulnerable people. They are a stark reminder of the human cost experienced when inter-professional collaboration is not effective in supporting and safeguarding individuals. The Munro review of child protection addressed inter-professional collaboration and made recommendations related to it. They include a new 'inspection framework that should examine the effectiveness of the contributions of all local services, including health, education, police, probation and the justice system to the protection of children' (Munro, 2011: 11).

Activity

Gather further information on the inquiries mentioned above and others. There are helpful summaries on internet websites. Read them to gain further details of the shortcomings and criticisms made. List these to see common threads.

Do you think lessons have not been learnt? List possible reasons for lack of collaboration between professionals and agencies.

A team around the service user

When a number of professionals and agencies are involved, it is appropriate to question whether this helps or hinders the service user. An assortment of workers may be bewildering and confusing for people who use their services. The result might be that 'too many cooks spoil the broth'. Alternatively, a network of help and support from a variety of professionals might be experienced as comforting and reassuring by the service user.

Contrasting applicable proverbs might be 'the more the merrier' or 'many hands make light work'.

Cheminais (2009) outlines the origin, concept and principles of a Team Around the Child (TAC) first advocated by Peter Limbrick, an independent consultant, in 2001. It 'is a model of service provision in which a range of different practitioners come together to help and support an individual child' (Cheminais, 2009: 70). 'TAC is designed to be an uncomplicated, appealing, common-sense, easily understood and non-threatening concept for parents, children and practitioners alike' (Cheminais, 2009: 71). It is ironic that an 'uncomplicated' and 'common-sense' concept seems so difficult to achieve, as evidenced by tragedies that have led to inquiries as discussed above.

Siraj-Blatchford et al. (2007) explore the concept further, outlining changes to children's services arising from the recommendations of inquiries and government responses, with a focus on multi-agency working in children's early years. TAC suggests a teamworking approach to inter-professional collaboration. The foreword by Dame Gillian Pugh (Pugh, 2007: ix) ends by acknowledging that:

> developing and maintaining good multi-agency working is not always easy, but, a team around the child, starting with the child, can create a service that is more responsive to the needs of individual children and their prents and which should give young children the best possible start in life.

The idea of a team around the service user, although applied to children in TAC, is just as valid for adult services and community care. In Chapter 2, we explored teams as systems, thus it is helpful to think in terms of service users having a support system or network around them. But such a system can only be perceived by a service user as helpful if it ensures the professionals involved understand the service user's circumstances and work together in a coordinated way to help meet identified needs.

The assessment jigsaw

Helm (2010) uses the analogy of a jigsaw to understand children's lives and assess their circumstances, notwithstanding the use of assessment tools and frameworks that do not necessarily have the flexibility to address the complexities of human beings and family life. The analogy suggests that in inter-professional assessments, you are putting together a jigsaw with no straight edges to provide boundaries and no picture on the box to show you what the finished jigsaw will look like. 'You have a picture emerging and you need to consider each new piece of the jigsaw to see where it fits and how the picture develops as new pieces are added' (Helm, 2010: 80). However, you do not have all the pieces in one place easily available to you. Parents and children usually hold the largest pieces of the picture, health visitors and teachers tend to hold key pieces, and social workers, the police and other agencies and professionals hold others.

This analogy, which also applies to adult services and community care, reminds us of the intricacy of assessing someone's situation and the need to coordinate information from a variety of sources to build a picture of the service user's circumstances. One person putting together an assessment jigsaw would find the task difficult but potentially manageable. When a number of professionals have contact with a service user, they all have some of the jigsaw pieces and are contributing to put it together. The team around the service user can itself be seen as a jigsaw.

Every social work assessment has an element of risk assessment and at times social workers are required to specifically assess risks such as the possibility of significant harm to a child or of an adult being a danger to themselves or others (Martin, 2010). An actuarial or statistical risk assessment relies on the probability of an event occurring based on past known risk factors. Professionals can use risk assessment tools that include probability factors. An alternative, and at times complementary, method is clinical assessment undertaken by professionals taking into account the background and individual circumstances of a service user. In clinical risk assessment, a number of factors specific to a service user have to be weighed and this inevitably introduces a subjective element.

When such risk assessment involves gathering information through interprofessional collaboration, it is again like putting together a jigsaw whose pieces are in the possession of a number of practitioners and agencies. Tragedies have resulted when such information has not been fully shared, brought together and analysed. It is important for a safeguarding strategy meeting to take place when required and for all professionals to attend. In urgent situations, there may a need for a 'virtual' meeting through telephone contact with relevant agencies, when arranging a meeting that professionals can attend would take too long.

Implications of cooperation

Munro's (2011) recommendations include ways of coordinating early intervention and strengthening child protection through developing social work expertise and making social work less bureaucratised and concerned with compliance. She recommends a review of health and social care partnership arrangements by government and medical colleges and the identification of the range of professional help available for the provision of local early help services.

The aim of such developments is to enhance the standing of social work practice and contextualise the importance of inter-professional teamworking. They point to the significance of social workers engaging in multi-agency partnership working, cooperating and communicating with other professionals, collaborating and sharing information about their involvement with common service users, and agreeing who will be responsible for particular areas of work. The participation and contribution of each professional should be clear. The appointment of a key worker or lead professional is important.

Something to guard against is diffusion of responsibility, which can be a side-effect of teamworking. We noted in Chapter 5 that decisions made by a group of individuals collectively are different from those that might be made by any individual member of the group. The group becomes responsible for the decision, rather than any of the individuals, with the danger of 'groupthink'. When the group involves the inter-professional collaboration of practitioners who are based in different geographical locations, the possibility of uncertain and diffuse responsibility is intensified.

Case example

A number of agencies were in contact with a mother and her 9-year-old daughter who often arrived late at school, grubby and dressed in shabby clothes. She appeared to have lost weight, to often be hungry and at times teachers noticed her asleep in class. There was a great deal of telephone and email contact between agencies. A health visitor said she was very worried about the mother's poor parenting skills. A school family liaison officer outlined concerns about standards in the home. A community psychiatric nurse suggested a change of social worker because the mother had told her that she did not like or get on with her social worker. Several professionals pointed out that the mother could be demanding and verbally aggressive and they were anxious when making home visits. There was reluctance from agencies to initiate a Common Assessment Framework (CAF) to share information. Emails to the social worker included questions such as 'can you do a CAF?' They added the opinion that 'it is not our job'.

The social worker called a professionals meeting to coordinate views and information and discuss a way forward. At the meeting, comments seemed to be mellowed and concerns minimised. The social worker was surprised that the tone of comments seemed very different from those shared by email and telephone. The health visitor said she thought the mother's parenting was good enough. The family liaison officer confirmed she had not visited the home. The community psychiatric nurse felt it was best for the social worker to continue monitoring the situation. However, following the meeting there were further telephone calls and emails expressing renewed concerns and worries not voiced at the meeting.

Factors contributing to poor inter-professional working

Sharkey (2007) explores structures that make it difficult for a variety of professional workers involved in the delivery of community care to work together, pointing out that 'Community care is rife with boundary, demarcation and funding disputes. This is partly responsible for the "maze" that the community care system can appear to be to service users and carers' (Sharkey, 2007: 183). He suggests four clusters of factors affecting poor inter-professional working:

1. The number of organisations involved.
2. Different structures making communication difficult.
3. Different budgets and financial arrangements.
4. Geographical boundaries.

The number of organisations involved is highlighted by the examples of Christopher Clunis and Victoria Climbié earlier in this chapter and by the individuals and agencies that had contact with them. In her review, Munro refers to the message from children (and their parents) that they value continuity in their relationships. This is difficult to achieve when many professionals are involved. She adds, 'For some children, there is also a problem of the bewildering large number of people who get involved in their case' (Munro, 2011: 32). Thus the number of organisations involved is hard for service users (children or adults) to relate to, as well a making it more difficult for all the organisations to work collaboratively together.

The structures of agencies range from the informality of some hostels and private care settings, through the independence of GP practices and the hierarchical organisation of hospitals with medical consultants that can be difficult to contact, to the bureaucracy of local authority social services directorates where lines of communication are sometimes rather rigid. It is difficult to achieve meaningful communication among varied professionals and particularly attendance of all participants at a coordinating or strategy meeting due to the number of individuals involved but also because of their styles of working, status and the structures of the organisations within which the various professionals work.

Different organisations have a variety of financial limits and priorities. Written evidence from the NHS Confederation to the House of Commons Health Committee in October 2011 commented on financial challenges faced by the NHS and stated:

> Pressure on local authority budgets is already having an impact on NHS services. In a major NHS Confederation survey of some 287 NHS chairs and CEOs, three quarters of respondents (75%) said cuts in local authority spending would definitely impact on their services in the next 12 months, predicting increased demand for community, mental health and primary care services. They also predicted increases in delayed discharges from hospital, acute admissions to hospital, emergency readmissions to hospital and A&E attendances.
>
> (Commons Health Select Committee, 2011)

It is not unknown for agencies to suggest another organisation should be allocated to work with a service user or for one of their practitioners to become the key worker because that organisation then becomes financially responsible, thus lightening the load on the other agency's budget, rather than the decision being made for the benefit of the service user taking into account who is the most appropriate professional and agency to work with them

The geographical boundaries of organisations that need to engage in interprofessional collaboration do not necessarily coincide. The majority of social workers are employed by local authorities but the team of which they are a part and their work base may be in a hospital, within an NHS health trust, specific mental health trust, GP attached, a new GP clinical commissioning group replacing a primary care trust, a health and wellbeing board or local health centre. Social workers may be seconded to specific work locations or be employed by an NHS trust. The geographical boundaries of these organisations can differ and it makes it particularly difficult to coordinate services for older and disabled people who have health and social care needs and those with mental health problems.

Activity

Consider a situation in your work with a service user where you have been involved in inter-professional collaboration with other practitioners and agencies as a social worker or student on placement. Make a list of who was involved.

Honestly assess how well you knew everyone concerned, their agency remit, geographical boundaries, powers and duties, roles and responsibilities. How did you communicate and keep in contact with them all?

There are no easy solutions to overcome the negative effects of the four factors affecting inter-professional working discussed above. Awareness of them can be a first step to ensuring that they do not completely obstruct inter-professional collaboration. As a social worker, you will need determination to maintain honest, open and regular communication with a number of professionals and agencies; work towards personal contacts overcoming structural obstacles; be creative and innovative in the funding of services; and work to the premise that different geographical boundaries do not necessarily have to create inter-professional barriers.

Professional boundaries may be as difficult to bridge as geographical ones. In the previous chapter, we explored characteristics of different professional disciplines that result in misunderstanding and unhelpful stereotypical perceptions. 'Organisational tribalism' and 'tribal allegiances' (Daley, 1989) lead to competition and mistrust. Many of the issues previously discussed regarding the strengths and weaknesses of team-working within an agency apply to a geographically scattered 'team'. It pays to get to know the professionals in the team around the service user, clarify mutual perceptions, responsibilities and roles. The risk thresholds of some professionals and agencies may differ from others, so the management of risk requires discussion and agreement about statutory, agency-specific and shared roles.

Case example

Ruby (aged 78) had been in hospital for three months. She had a malignant growth pushing down on her womb. A suspected perforated uterus caused occasional bleeding. As she had mild learning difficulties, a health professional from the NHS Safeguarding Team had made an assessment that she had the capacity, under the 2005 Mental Capacity Act (MCA), to refuse an operation. As she was a vulnerable person, an independent advocate had been appointed. Professionals found it difficult to discuss her circumstances and ascertain her wishes because she refused to answer most questions. She said she wanted to stay in hospital but it was assessed that she did not have the capacity to make that decision.

To discuss plans, a 'best interest' meeting was held chaired by a social work senior practitioner under the MCA to make a decision on Ruby's behalf in her best interests. Members of her family were invited to the meeting for consultation but would not contribute to the decision. A medical consultant expressed the view that Ruby should go into residential care.

Prior to her hospital stay Ruby had lived in a sheltered housing flat for some years and she was very familiar with that accommodation. A residential home would be a new environment unfamiliar to Ruby and it was noted that she found it very difficult to cope with change. Although the social work senior practitioner did not have the medical knowledge and understanding of a prognosis to the level of the consultant, she discussed with him the social and emotional impact of Ruby going to a new residential care setting and disagreed with the consultant. In chairing she attempted to focus on Ruby as a vulnerable person lacking the capacity to make a decision.

Organisational systems vs. people

Central and local governments regularly restructure services such as health and social care with stated objectives usually including increased partnership working and improved outcomes for service users. However, restructuring seldom results in significant improvements. In a government studies policy paper, Glasby (2012: 4) points out that 'Structural change by itself rarely achieves stated objectives.' Payne (2000: 148) reminds us that 'Crucially, organisational systems do not create cooperation, people do.'

Hudson (2002) reviews literature sceptical of joint working that takes a pessimistic view of what he terms 'inter-professionality' due to factors such as those reviewed above. However, based on a study of GPs, community nurses and social workers in the north of England, he puts forward an optimistic analysis of what is possible.

Implications for practice

Since people are crucial to cooperation, this chapter takes an optimistic view and now moves, as the previous chapter did, to consider skills and actions that need to be taken by professionals, the qualities of the professional as a person, and underpinning professional values that influence how skills are used in inter-professional and multi-agency collaboration. These characteristics are explored under the following headings:

- Mindset and professional attitude
- Role and responsibilities
- Inter-professional collaboration

Mindset and professional attitude

The Professionalism PCF domain states that from being a social work student on practice placements you should 'Demonstrate professionalism in terms of presentation, demeanour, reliability, honesty and respectfulness', and the Contexts and Organisations domain states that as a newly qualified worker you should 'Proactively engage with colleagues, and a range of organisations to identify, assess, plan and support the needs of service users and communities' (The College of Social Work, 2012). These requirements suggest a starting point in professional collaboration to present yourself as a capable and reliable professional.

For a collaborative mindset, it would help you to think systemically about the number of professionals and agencies you are working with in meeting the needs of a service user. Another, related, way of thinking is to see yourself as part of a team around the service user. As an integral part of a system (discussed in Chapter 2) you should be aware of connections between individuals and sub-systems and work towards these contributing in a positive way to achieve agreed outcomes. Play your part in networking and opening boundaries. Contribute towards establishing a stable system but flexible team with room for some individual autonomy, tolerant of disagreement, open to learning and to the development of new work patterns, not set in the traditions of different professional disciplines.

Ensure you know who is involved in the team around the service user. Get to know other services and their procedures. Work to overcome set boundaries. Notwithstanding the apparently inevitable organisational restructuring that you or other professionals are likely to regularly experience, contribute to restructuring relationships between different professional disciplines so that collaboration becomes the norm. Be positive, taking an optimistic view of inter-professional collaboration, rather than the pessimistic approach which questions whether it is possible to cooperate with practitioners from diverse professional disciplines.

Role and responsibilities

The Professionalism PCF domain states that as a newly qualified worker you should 'Be able to explain the role of the social worker in a range of contexts, and uphold the reputation of the profession' (The College of Social Work, 2012). When working inter-professionally, you can contribute your social work skills, knowledge and values and see yourself as a representative, acting on behalf of your agency. Be assertive in your social work role and an advocate for service users.

Clarify your role in the teamworking approach to meeting a service user's needs and also clarify how your role and responsibilities fit in with those of others. Roles should include responsibility for assessment, planning, implementation and review. Agree the boundaries of your role and who is accountable for outcomes. Roles and responsibilities can overlap and be shared by more than one professional but, if this is so, they need to be clear, not diffused. Guard particularly against diffusion of responsibility.

Responsibilities can be allocated according to expertise. Not every professional will have direct contact with the service user. A role you might undertake, for instance, is that of consultant to another practitioner. Seek agreement on who takes leadership for which tasks. It is important that one practitioner should be the key worker or lead professional.

Inter-professional collaboration

Communication is key to collaboration, something that can start with fundamental practical needs such as having the names, telephone numbers and email addresses of all professionals involved with a service user. Ensure that you attend strategy, coordinating and review meetings. General networking also contributes to collaboration, so it would help you to attend more general professional gatherings and events whenever possible.

Like a jigsaw, in assessment and planning you will be contributing to building a picture of the service user's circumstances. Gather and share information and coordinate decisions. Use your assessment skills but involve other practitioners when making professional judgements such as those needed for clinical risk assessment. The building of interpersonal relationships with other professionals is crucial. Regular contact and liaison can overcome structural and organisational differences and boundaries. Get to know other professionals and take an interest in their disciplines. This will help overcome differences in priorities, language and jargon. Avoid negative stereotypes and power struggles.

Contribute to clarifying tasks and objectives. Identify any gaps in what the inter-professional team is offering a service user and make these known. Keep the service user at the centre of the process. Involve and include the service user, explaining procedures, informing them about the role of various professionals and ensuring they participate, including attending meetings.

Chapter summary

Having explored aspects of multidisciplinary collaboration within a team in the previous chapter, this one focused on the extent to which a number of professionals from different agencies can collaborate and create a team around the service user. The chapter started with a reminder of the messages from inquiries into tragedies over the years that have highlighted unclear responsibilities and accountability, poor communication, inadequate planning and coordination of services, and lack of collaboration and information sharing between agencies.

The chapter explored the concept of a team around the service user but acknowledged that the assessment of service users' needs and risks is difficult when a number of professionals are involved, likening this to a complex, unbounded and unclear assessment jigsaw. We stressed the need for coordination and the importance of guarding against diffusion of responsibility, which can be a side-effect of teamworking. The chapter considered factors contributing to poor inter-professional working such as the number of organisations involved, different structures, budgets and financial arrangements, geographical boundaries and professional boundaries, which might be difficult to bridge. While accepting there are no easy solutions, we noted that awareness of the factors and determination to overcome them are important, remembering that people, rather than systems, can create cooperation.

As in the previous chapter, this one outlined skills, actions, qualities and values needed for inter-professional collaboration under the categories of 'mindset and professional attitude', 'roles and responsibilities' and 'inter-professional collaboration' itself.

Further reading

Crawford, K. (2012) *Interprofessional Collaboration in Social Work Practice*. London: Sage. This textbook aims to help the reader understand collaborative practice and consider professional practice in the collaborative environment. It has elements of a workbook, with many activities, reflective questions and other exercises to engage the reader.

Morris, K. (ed.) (2008) *Social Work and Multi-agency Working: Making a Difference*. Bristol: The Policy Press. Following a chapter setting the scene, a variety of contributors explore multi-agency working with eight service user groups, including youth justice, children and families, mental health, drug problems, learning disabilities and older people.

9   Teamwork as a student

Introduction

Although this chapter comes towards the end of the book, it will be of particular interest and use if you are a social work student yet to experience some of the teamworking situations outlined in previous chapters. This chapter will consider collaborative working as part of a year cohort of students, in formal and informal small group work projects that are often part of learning and assessment, and when you become part of a team in a practice placement.

The student experience

As a student starting a social work qualifying degree programme you will probably wonder what the experience is going to be like. It is likely that you will be excited but also anxious. You may speculate about the characters, backgrounds and experience of your fellow students at least until you get to know them as the course progresses. When discussing expectations at the beginning of the programme, social work students often include the hope that they will work 'as a team' supporting each other and collaborating in their studying and learning. Given the intake numbers for new cohorts of students, which can range from perhaps forty or so to over 100, it is unlikely that you will be a 'team' as we envisaged it in Chapter 2. However, you will experience interdependence, a mix of complementary skills and roles among your fellow students and some collaborative working towards the ultimate goal: to successfully complete the degree and obtain a social work qualification – thus, by definition, there will be elements of teamworking as a social work student.

In some sessions, you may be in smaller groups of students and your course may require your participation in small group work projects and presentations, whether assessed or not, when the characteristics and dynamics of teamworking will be part of your experience.

Stages during the life of a student cohort

As a year cohort, although probably part of a large number of students, you may well experience some of the stages discussed in Chapter 3. Students can be said to be 'forming' towards the beginning of the programme when unsure of expectations, routines and accepted ways of behaving, relating to each other and to tutors. You may start university having previously been at school or college and find the expectations different and the level of study a step up from what you are used to, making you apprehensive. You may be starting the degree programme following years of life experience but not having been in full-time education for some time. Becoming a university student may feel strange and make you anxious. Interaction with as many of your fellow students as possible and with tutors and lecturers will help you with this stage. The university expectation is that you are an adult responsible for your learning, which may make you feel as if you are alone tackling your studies. However, the university tradition is also that students work in partnership with members of staff and with each other.

As you participate in the programme, there may well be times when you experience uncertainty, pressure and a feeling that the course is overwhelming. You may wonder whether you will be able to cope. It may seem to you that other students are doing better and are more able than you; but others may feel the same about you! Student sub-groups may form, which may provide some support but can be experienced as exclusive. Receiving the first assessment results can be a turbulent time when you wonder whether to compare marks with others, celebrate quietly, or despair due to a disappointing grade. All this can result in examples of 'storming', such as tensions between fellow students and resentment towards staff. These are times to seek and accept the support of other students, tutors and other university services, have honest discussions, set yourself goals and look forward to the next stage of the programme.

Getting to know requirements and establishing patterns of student life can be seen as 'norming'. You will settle into study routines, subjects may start to make sense and you will probably make links between different modules so that you feel as if you are pursuing a 'joined up' course. You learn to learn and share ways of tackling the programme with fellow students. You may find that lecturers and tutors are more helpful than demanding. As the course progresses, you start to feel that you will be able to succeed. Sharing these experiences with other students provides mutual help and supports your progress.

Coping with the challenges of the programme and meeting the academic and practice requirements will lead to 'performing'. You will have the success of passing each year or stage and proceeding to the next. As you are undertaking a professional as well as an academic qualification, you may increasingly feel that you are acquiring a professional social work identity. Starting practice placements can launch you onto a fresh round of forming, storming and norming stages but they usually also lead to performing with a sense that you are demonstrating your capability through putting skills into practice.

The achievement of results will take you to the 'ending' stage with a feeling of accomplishment but probably also a sense of regret and loss that you will be disbanding and going your separate ways, even if you keep in touch with a number of fellow students. The ending of each practice placement can be significant with feelings of achievement and relief but also possible sadness at ending your involvement with practitioners. Every ending is the start of a new beginning, whether it is back to university or becoming a newly qualified social worker. This is a reminder that stages involve a personal and professional developmental sequence.

During the course there may be some functional roles open to you, such as becoming a year representative on a staff/student consultative group. These roles tend to be few within a degree programme but there are certainly 'team' roles that each individual student can contribute depending on your learning style (e.g. a doer activist, thinking reflector, intellectual theorist, or planner pragmatist) and on your behaviour and personality (e.g. carer, creative, questioner, leader, achiever). These roles influence the student group dynamics and are experienced mainly as positive contributions within a 'performing' group.

Personal and cultural factors

Your approach to learning will also depend on factors such as your age, previous experience of education, cultural values and ethnicity. If you have joined the course from school or college, being given responsibility for your own learning and how you tackle academic assignments may be new to you. Alternatively, your previous experience of education may be from another country and culture where you expect to be taught by an expert instructor and your cultural tradition is that you respect lecturers as elders. This is typical, for instance, of most African cultures.

In my experience during quite a number of years as a university lecturer and social work tutor, I often found that many Black African students called me 'sir', treated me with respect bordering on deference to authority and some said that they saw me as a 'father' figure. This was something I did not seek or expect and I would at times tell students that there was no need for them to treat me in such a way. However, I accepted it as the cultural tradition that many students brought to the programme.

Another African and Asian cultural tradition is 'collectivism' as opposed to the white western tradition of 'individualism'. Gushue and Constantine (2003) researched individualism, collectivism and self-differentiation in African American college women and Vogt and Laher (2009) conducted a study with South African university students comparing individualism/collectivism with other personality factors proposed by psychologists. Such studies suggest that individualism and collectivism are cultural differences and relate to a self-concept rather than personality traits. Students steeped in the tradition of 'individualism' are more likely to value independence and self-reliance and pursue personal goals.

A collectivism cultural tradition, relating to values of kinship, community and 'nation as a family' resonate with teamworking as we noted in Chapter 4. Your cultural background may enable you to contribute to group goals among students, promoting interdependence but you may have to learn to develop a more individual personal responsibility for your own learning, not totally relying on fellow students or on the authority of lecturers and tutors to teach you knowledge and skills.

Reflection

Reflect on your current or previous experience as a social work student.

- What stages can you identify that you went through and what particular roles did you play?
- How did your previous experience, background and culture impact on your studies?
- Did you experience any of your participation on a social work programme as team-working? If so, in what ways?

Creating your own student team

As you get to know other students, form friendships and discover common interests, you may decide to get together informally with a small group of fellow students to discuss ideas put forward by lecturers and tutors, pool resources to gather information, offer each other mutual help and support, and perhaps work together on course assignments. As a team you can research topics together, stimulate thinking and generate new ideas, thus creating a helpful study culture. Textbooks can be difficult to come by due to the expense of buying them and finite supplies in libraries, however well stocked, so sharing books and reading materials and letting each other know about different sources of information can be a useful form of collaboration.

While such activities amount to good teamwork, a note of caution is also appropriate. We have already noted that you are responsible for your own learning, so it is important to keep in mind that any academic work must be your own. Collaboration and mutual support is to be commended but not copying or producing material that is uniform rather than showing evidence of your learning, understanding and original work. Plagiarism includes reproducing as your own the work of other authors, other students and extracts from any assignment that you have previously submitted.

When working as a study team, there is also a danger that you might be tempted to compare yourself with other students and feel they are coping better with study than you are. As far as course requirements and assignment guidelines are concerned, always consult official information and, if uncertain, ask tutors for clarification. It is surprising how erroneous myths and misinformation regarding requirements and expectations can spread when interacting with other students. These messages pass from one student to another and you believe them to be true. The aim of coming together as an informal study team must be to mutually reinforce learning rather than obscure understanding.

Small group work as a student

In most if not all social work degree programmes, you will at times be required to offi-
cially work in small groups to prepare a presentation or undertake a project. Ideally you
will be working as a team in these instances to achieve the required outcome. There is
unlikely to be an appointed team leader, so you will have to be aware of the roles
various students, including you, play, such as taking a lead to suggest meetings, how to
allocate responsibilities among team members, set goals and agree targets toward the
stated task.

In an effective team, members accept interdependence, collaborate with one
another and keep each other informed of progress. However, this may not always
happen and there can be power struggles, disagreements and tensions. Some of these
can be due to stereotypical expectations based on factors such as gender, age, personality and ethnicity. The work you are planning may be assessed and a group mark is
sometimes given for part or all of the assessment. It can be very frustrating and annoying
if any team members miss planning meetings or fail to do their allocated portion of the
work. The feeling is that one or more team members are not 'pulling their weight' or
'letting the side down'. Alternatively, someone may dominate discussions and try to
impose their ideas. As with most aspects of life, learning issues have emotional
overtones.

Case example

As part of a Social Policy module on the first year of their Social Work degree, students had
to form small groups, choose a topic and prepare a presentation that would contribute to
the assessment of the module. Evie, a student in her 40s, had established a relationship with
one of the youngest students on the course, Amy, and tended to support her a good deal
in an almost motherly way. Amy was friendly with Katelyn, so when the topics were distributed the three of them who were sitting together immediately decided to form a group.
Aaliyah, who was sitting nearby, asked to join them and they agreed. It was not until nearly
the end of the session that they noticed Tony who had not yet decided on a group and,
feeling sorry for him, they invited him to join. They agreed to meet the following week after
a lecture.

Although they were looking forward to starting the project, most of them found the first
meeting difficult because they had different expectations of what was required. Evie tended
to take a lead and relate the topic and the information they had to gather to her years of
experience working in residential care. Amy was concerned that they should follow the
guidelines and repeatedly referred to them wondering whether they should seek clarification. Katelyn was very jovial, which annoyed some of the others, as she did not seem to be
taking the task seriously. Aaliyah had not been brought up in this country and felt at a slight
disadvantage due to her perception that she was not very familiar with the Welfare State
and British Government policy. Tony tended to take a more theoretical approach and

wanted them all to get books from the library. In a meeting that lasted much longer than they anticipated, they finally agreed that each of them would research one aspect of the topic.

Katelyn sent apologies for their next meeting but they were surprised that she had already started preparing PowerPoint slides, emailed them to the rest of the group and seemed to have gone beyond the remit that she had agreed to focus on and had included slides on areas that others had been researching. Evie had not done as much research as she hoped but relied on her experience again in discussion. Tony felt somewhat excluded as the only male and because his perception was that the others were not willing to work to the academic level that he thought the project demanded. Aaliyah sensed this and attempted to involve him in discussion and reach a compromise about the approach to take. This meeting felt like two sub-groups or pairs, Evie and Amy on one side and Aaliyah and Tony on the other, who found their views difficult to reconcile.

There were two more planning meetings when other group members could not attend due to commitments, many emails backward and forwards, and the presentation date was fast approaching. Through email contact they found a date that they could all attend and Aaliyah took a lead suggesting they devote most of that meeting to discussion of how they were relating to each other and whether they were working as a team, agreeing that each could honestly say how they were feeling while respecting each other's views. This did help them to progress and, following more planning eventually the presentation went quite well. They met afterwards for a coffee to celebrate and at that informal and relaxed gathering they were able to share some understanding of each other's positions in a way that had not been possible during meetings to plan the presentation.

To work as a team in a small formal or informal student group, you will need good communication skills and a willingness to discuss difficulties and disagreements openly and honestly within the group even though this may be hard and uncomfortable. You will also need to keep in mind that teamworking is collaborative, so your aim is to cooperate rather than feel that you are in competition with your fellow students. It is more helpful to voice your opinions objectively in planning meetings than to sit in silence indicating passive aggression or disinterest. Communicating through email is especially appropriate when it is difficult to arrange mutually convenient meetings. However, group members need to use emails constructively to share information, not to be critical and vent feelings.

Through both positive and negative experiences you will learn about teamworking, and you will develop skills as a student that you can use to participate in teams in practice placements and eventually as a qualified social worker. In a social work degree programme for which I was a tutor, a small group project was used to gather information about interdisciplinary collaboration and multi-agency working focusing on specific service user groups. Part of the assessment was an individual reflective account by each student of their experience within the small group, making parallels between that experience and professionals from different disciplines collaborating in work with service users. Whether a specific learning outcome of the programme or not, you can relate your experience of small group work as a student to cooperation in multidisciplinary teams and inter-professional collaboration as discussed in the previous two chapters.

Practice learning opportunities

Once you have been allocated a placement to undertake practice learning, you will join an agency work team. Although you will have a practice educator and, in some cases, a separate on-site supervisor, a good model for the agency providing the placement and something you are entitled to expect is that your practice learning opportunities are with the team, not merely with an individual practitioner. At least part of your learning will arise from the experience of being a team member and you will have the expertise and knowledge of all members of the team for your support and development. Content from previous chapters is relevant for you to understand and participate in your placement team and to be aware of teamworking skills that you should develop.

As a student on placement you may, at least initially, feel uncertain, lacking knowledge and experience and your perception might be that you are a junior team member, 'just a student' with low status and little if anything to contribute. You can counteract such feelings and perceptions by developing relationships with all team members and remembering that you also contribute experience and knowledge to the team. You were successful in obtaining a place in your degree programme, so through the selection process you were assessed as being ready to undertake training and as having the potential to become a professional social worker. You will bring your university teaching and learning prior to the start of the placement, which may be more up to date than that of other team members.

There will be an agreement for you to have regular individual supervision sessions but you can also look to others in the team to provide you with supervision, support and practice teaching. For this to be effective, you need to be proactive in engaging with all members of the team and getting to know their interests and expertise.

Case example

Olivia's first placement on her social work degree programme was with a Youth Offending Team (YOT). She was eager and somewhat apprehensive when she started. She was surprised at how large the team was with about twenty-five practitioners and five administrative, secretarial and reception staff, so thirty people to get to know. Being a multidisciplinary team there were a variety of professionals, from social work, probation, police, health, education and many other workers with specific remits to get to know and ask about their work. YOT was a new area for Olivia and there had been little mention of it in the university teaching thus far, so she welcomed her induction with a considerable amount of written material to read but also time to spend with the various members of the team. They were welcoming and happy to discuss their work with her.

She found that practitioners worked closely with the service users, seeing them individually and in groups, in a games room at the back of the building and often mixing with them informally while making a drink before meeting. She noticed that the young people moved freely around the building and, once past the front door reception and security lock, there were very few restrictions to their movement. She assessed the YOT ethos and team culture as informal but keeping to statutory requirements, supportive, inclusive and interested in training and professional development.

Her practice educator was a social worker who suggested she attend Court regularly on agreed days after induction. Olivia found herself working closely with a Court 'sub-team' within YOT. A bail and remand officer discussed her experiences after Court hearings in a helpful way that amounted to informal supervision, while she continued regular weekly formal supervision with her practice educator. Her first attendance at a monthly full team meeting was daunting due to the number of people involved. She found it interesting and informative but did not contribute. At other smaller meetings, with an intensive work 'sub-team' and in a risk meeting, she felt increasingly able to participate and was encouraged to do so. Her practice educator suggested she should do a 15-minute presentation at a full team meeting, giving her two months notice, on a topic she had researched for an assignment at university.

Some placements are in community, day and residential care settings without a traditional social work ethos. There may not be a qualified social worker in the team you join. You will nevertheless be able to learn and practise transferable knowledge and skills. It is important to use the support of your off-site practice educator to develop your role in the team and your social work identity. You may face the dilemma of being asked not to introduce yourself as a social work student or social worker in training in settings such as a family centre where many parents have had negative experiences with social workers and show antipathy towards anything to do with social work. There is no right or wrong answer about this but, discussing it within the team, you can explore the issues, voice your opinion and agree a way forward.

Tension within your placement team

We have seen in previous chapters that human interaction within teams can at times produce tension, friction and misunderstandings. You may come across this in the team that you are part of during your placement. It is possible that you will experience interactions between team members that are emotionally charged, power dynamics and positioning. Not all team communication is open and honest and at an Adult-to-Adult level. We noted in Chapter 2 that the transactions of professionals can at times be from a forceful critical or controlling parent or from a weak adapted child ego state. In multidisciplinary teams, there may be disagreements influenced by stereotypical assumptions about different professions or due to clashes of perceived status. You may experience storming but, as we noted in Chapter 3, it might be helpful for you to distinguish the difference between the storming of an immature team and the 'challenge and change' that is possible in a mature team where members understand and respect each other.

You will experience team members in your placement playing a variety of roles. It is useful for you to be aware of this and observe the contributions that team members make within their roles; discussing this with them can in fact be a good learning experience. However, while in this book we have focused mainly on positive roles, with allowable weaknesses, we have also mentioned more negative ones. You may come across the critical, hard to please team member, demanding and inflexible ones and forceful challengers. It can become uncomfortable when team members involve you in their unhelpful interaction. Someone may gossip, criticise or give you inappropriate information about another member of the team. During tense exchanges, a 'persecutor' may attempt to put you in the role of 'victim' feeling that if they didn't have to be looking after a student they could concentrate on other more important matters. You might be the recipient of displaced frustrations or anger.

Dealing with such situations is difficult. A first port of call is always to discuss such matters if they arise with your practice educator. It is best to be open, candid and straightforward in raising issues with your practice educator. In more extreme circumstances, you may want to contact your university tutor or, ultimately, follow an agreed complaints or whistleblowing procedure. This is likely to be a last resort.

It is advisable to write down your experiences. Keeping a reflective diary is a useful learning tool in placement and you can reflect on positive as well as on negative critical incidents. Although experiencing team tension is uncomfortable, you can learn from it and use skills to manage conflict as previously discussed. When dealing with emotionally charged situations, developing your emotional intelligence and resilience will enhance your professionalism.

Assessment concerns

Most students enjoy their practice opportunities and learn much from them. Your practice educator and the whole team will want you to pass the placement and will be supporting you and looking for ways of enabling you to do so. However, your practice educator could believe that you have not shown evidence of the capabilities against which you are assessed. The practice educator may have assessed weaknesses in your practice and warn you that you could fail the placement.

Even at such difficult times it is helpful to regard your placement as being with the team not just with your individual practice educator. You may be tempted to hide the assessment from the rest of the team and only discuss it with your practice educator. However, a plan of action to address your weaknesses should involve other members of the team. Some of the evidence for your capability can come from them. The more sources of evidence you have to put forward, the better informed your practice educator's assessment will be.

Chapter summary

This chapter has explored aspects of teamwork that you are likely to encounter as a social work student. It considered collaborative working as part of a year cohort and in informal and formal small group work projects. In reflecting on the student experience, the chapter applied typical stages of a team's life to a larger student cohort and suggested you may experience 'forming' while adjusting to university and wondering about routines and expectations; 'storming' such as tensions between fellow students and resentment towards staff when there are pressures and demands; 'norming' through getting to know requirements and establishing patterns of student life; 'performing' when coping with the challenges of the programme and meeting the academic and practice requirements; and 'ending' with a feeling of achievement but some regret and a sense of loss at disbanding.

It was suggested that students may play team roles and that these are dependent on learning styles, behaviour and personality. We noted that your approach to learning will also depend on factors such as your age, previous experience of education, cultural values and ethnicity. The chapter proposed that cultural traditions such as the African and Asian 'collectivism' may enable some students to contribute to team goals promoting interdependence, but pointed out that you may have to learn to develop to take personal responsibility for your own learning, not relying on fellow students or on the authority of lecturers and tutors to teach you knowledge and skills.

Considering small group work and projects, the chapter explored aspects of working as a team, with its advantages and difficulties, providing opportunities to collaborate with other students, and learn and develop teamworking skills. The chapter also considered being part of work teams in practice placements and the need to participate fully. It explored the possibility of experiencing tensions in placement teams and ways of managing them. Finally, the chapter emphasised the importance of regarding the placement as being with the team, even if you find yourself in the difficult situation of your practice educator assessment highlighting weaknesses in your practice and the danger of you failing the placement.

Further reading

There is no specific textbook focusing solely on experiencing teamwork as a student. The two below explore aspects of being a social work student, so reinforce some of the areas covered in this chapter with implications for teamworking, even if not specifically highlighting them.

Lomax, R., Jones, K., Leigh, S. and Gay, C. (2010) *Surviving Your Social Work Placement.* Basingstoke: Palgrave Macmillan.

Walker, H. (2008) *Studying for your Social Work Degree*. Exeter: Learning Matters.

10 Conclusion

Having read through this book, or perhaps dipped into various parts of it, you may agree by now that teamwork is multifaceted and complex, and teamworking skills are varied and mostly not intuitive and thus need to be developed. The complexity can arise due to both the diversity of professional groups that we might regard as a 'team' and the intricate system of human interaction that teams represent. Diverse skills include those related to professionalism, self-management, critical reflection and analysis, and interpersonal relationships. Teams can range from a relatively small number of social workers in one work location to a much larger number of geographically scattered practitioners from different professional disciplines or agencies. We started to consider such an assortment of characteristics and issues in Chapter 1 when introducing areas that the book would address, the approach the book would take and how you could interact with it.

In addition to reviewing definitions, highlighting the importance of teams and the concept of 'synergy' – a team being able to achieve more than the sum of its individual members – Chapter 2 introduced a number of theoretical ideas. Psychodynamic unconscious processes, transference and defence mechanisms help us to understand possible internal conflict within us as individuals and how we relate to others. Transactional analysis is a useful theoretical model to explain human interaction. It can promote self-awareness and provides useful concepts to assess the nature of relationships within a team generally and, more specifically, our own relationship with other individual team members. It can point to the danger of dominant and dependent individuals within a team and reminds us that Adult-to-Adult objective and professional communication is the aim.

An ecological approach and systemic analysis helps us understand the team as a whole within its wider contexts. Teams function within and are influenced by a national macro context of government initiatives, legislation, requirements and social work developments and trends. Teams are part of a meso landscape of regional networks, local authorities and organisational environments. It is important to be aware of and familiar with these macro and meso influences and to work purposefully within them. At the micro level, teams themselves are interconnected systems with more or less permeable boundaries and inner dynamics relating to individual team members. Teams can be experienced as chaotic, conforming or flexible.

A self-rating activity (see pp. 117–18) is included to help you assess how your team measures up to the characteristics outlined in Chapter 2, encouraging you to list evidence for your answers. As previously stated, you can do this on your own but it might be more productive to undertake the activity with your team colleagues, individually at first and then moving on to compare notes. This is likely to generate useful discussion about each team member's understanding of the characteristics and the evidence they draw upon to support their rating. The exercise itself may help develop the team through identifying characteristics such as those relating to what kind of a team you are and relationships between team members. You can enter into discussion to find ways of promoting these characteristics, particularly ones that need strengthening.

When you get to know a team, especially if it is a well-established one, you may become aware of a particular and distinct character that distinguishes it from other teams. It may be argued that a team can have its own personality, dependent on how it operates, the type of interactions between team members, cohesiveness and ability to meet demands and achieve results. The focus of Chapter 3 was to explore teams as distinct entities, having a life of their own. It considered a team's development towards maturity and beyond, reviewing models suggesting that groups, and teams, experience typical stages over time.

Chapter 3 noted stages that can also apply to team meetings. These can occasionally take some time to get going and include friction and tension but usually establish ways of moving forward towards positive outcomes leading to a satisfactory ending, rather than a frustrating sense of unfinished business. Considering power issues within teams, it is helpful to be aware of the difference between the 'storming' of an immature team and the 'challenge and change' that is possible in a mature team where members understand and respect each other.

We explored a model in which ingredients contributing to successful team functioning can be envisaged as three equal and overlapping circles representing needs related to achieving the team's task, building and maintaining the team, and meeting the individual needs of each team member. This is an ideal balance usually found in a mature and performing team. However, difficulties and disputes can arise among team members and these are best dealt with by discussing them openly and frankly as a team, although in extreme circumstances independent mediation external to the team may be advisable.

Focusing on individual team members, Chapter 4 highlighted their characteristics, suggesting that having a variety of complementary roles is better than uniformity. The chapter distinguished between functional roles, related to a person's title, job description and position in the organisation, and team roles, dependent on an individual's behaviour, personality and character. We noted that team roles have 'allowable weaknesses' such as a team worker who is cooperative but regarded by some as indecisive, or a challenger who urges the team to question established practices and decisions being perceived as easily provoked or capable of offending other people. Leadership is a functional role but can also be a team role shared by some or all team members.

The varied contributions that members playing different roles bring to a team have implications for new members joining a team and established members leaving it. Where possible, it is advisable to seek new members or replace those who have left with particular characteristics and team roles needed by the team. Chapter 4 also highlighted the importance of ensuring that all relevant individuals, including administrative, secretarial and support staff, are included within the boundary of team membership. The focus on individual team members led to exploration of the importance of emotional intelligence and resilience, and of self-leadership and personal development.

It is difficult to consider teamworking skills in isolation without also paying attention to the character and ethos of the team within which your skills are practised, your personal qualities as an individual team member, and a professional value base underpinning teamworking. Chapter 5 therefore reviewed skills within this wider context also referring to relevant PCF domains (The College of Social Work, 2012). The skills checklist included (p. 62–3) can be regarded as a chapter summary and is intended for you to rate your capability relating to each skill and plan ways of developing those skills where you score yourself low. This is of course an individual exercise that demands self-awareness and an honest appraisal. It might be salutary to also ask one or more team colleagues to complete it about you. Such an exercise could lead to a range of conclusions, including:

- your self-assessment being reassuringly in line with how colleagues perceive you;
- showing that you are too modest, underestimating your capability, and that colleagues rate you more highly than you do yourself;
- perceiving yourself as more skilled than your fellow workers rate you – this third possibility is arguably the most concerning.

The aim of the second part of the book is to apply aspects of teamwork and team-working skills to practice situations such as working in organisations, being a member of a multidisciplinary team, collaborating with other professionals and experiencing teamwork as a student.

The eighth PCF domain, Contexts and Organisations (The College of Social Work, 2012), addresses the capability to operate effectively within your organisation and contribute to it, 'team working' and working with others. Focusing on these expectations, Chapter 6 explored teams in organisations, from traditional structures to informal systems and open networks. To engage with your organisation, it is important to be aware of organisational and team culture, and the importance of service user and carer participation.

A systemic analysis about working in organisations ideally leads to an optimistic approach that contributes to achieving the goal of creating a 'learning organisation' culture. This entails individuals and teams developing their knowledge and skills and sharing them with others in the organisation, thus becoming a 'community of practice'. This is far more positive than perceiving the organisation, or its senior management, as making uninformed and unreasonable demands on you and feeling that you have little or no influence on organisational policy and expectations. Chapter 6 acknowledged the need for individual and team responsibility, accountability and liability. Teamworking with the benefit of regular supervision, including group and team supervision, can enable you through your team to become constructively engaged with your organisation.

Teamworking within a multidisciplinary team can potentially be more difficult than as part of a group of social work qualified colleagues due to the need to interact with practitioners that have different training, traditional ways of working, cultures, jargon, ethos and values. Chapter 7 addressed such tensions and the balance between multidisciplinary teams engaging in a new way of working conceptualised as a meta-discipline, within which there may be disciplinary strands, and safeguarding the identity and particular contribution of social work. Ways of resolving this dilemma include avoiding stereotypes, understanding the language and culture of other disciplines, working towards inclusion to avoid negative power dynamics, paying attention to how decisions are made and promoting service user and carer participation. The chapter outlined skills necessary for multidisciplinary teamworking, including those related to self-management, professionalism, interaction and collaboration with team colleagues and networking.

The track record of social workers communicating and collaborating with other professionals, coordinating services and sharing information is rather poor, as evidenced by inquiries into tragedies that have resulted in deaths. Barriers and obstacles to collaboration may relate to the number of organisations involved, their different structures, budgets and geographical boundaries. A variety of different professionals can be involved with an individual or family with no sense of them becoming a team around the service user.

While acknowledging that assessment, particularly inter-professional and multi-agency assessment, can be regarded as a complex jigsaw that has to be put together, Chapter 8 focused on the service provision concept of a team around the service user, starting with the service user, as common sense, uncomplicated and more responsive to need. An optimistic view suggests that people can work together purposefully rather than relying on organisational systems to promote joint working. The chapter outlined relevant skills, including those related to one's mindset and professional attitude, clear role and responsibilities, and inter-professional collaboration.

The application of teamworking skills to practice situations is also relevant to the experience of being a social work student, since students work collaboratively as a year cohort or in smaller groups and join work teams when on practice placements. Chapter 9 pointed out that a cohort of students progressing through the course can experience forming, storming, norming and performing, leading to ending stages reminiscent of those that teams can go through. Students getting together informally for study and mutual support or in formal small group projects can experience varying dynamics, tensions, power struggles and disagreements that previous chapters explored, but can also work effectively as a team.

The experience of teamwork in practice placements is similar to that of social workers and other professionals with the added complication that a student may, particularly at first, feel a 'junior', less experienced member of the team and has the concern and apprehension of being assessed on their capability. If you are a student, your practice educator has the responsibility at the end of your placement to recommend whether you pass or fail. An important message in Chapter 9 is for students to relate to all team members and see the placement as being with the team rather than an individual practice educator.

Reflection

At this stage of engaging with this textbook, it might be appropriate to stop and reflect.

- How are you experiencing teamwork currently, or how have you experienced it in previous work or study situations?
- How does being a member of a team make you feel?

Think teamwork

Whatever your previous and current experience, this textbook will have achieved one of its purposes if it helps you to 'think teamwork'. This might include considerations such as:

- Are you doing something that others in the team should know about? This might include a work project, professional activity or using specific assessment, planning intervention and evaluation tools.
- Are you working in a way that might be of interest to other team members? You might be using a particular theoretical model or you might be tackling issues with a service user in a way that has led you to think afresh.
- Have you come across organisations or individuals that others in your team might also benefit from contacting at some point?
- Have you found literature, a new book, a journal article, an internet site that you could share with others in the team?

If any of the above apply, you could send an email or a short note to colleague team members, you could ask for a slot in a team meeting or suggest a separate training or information sharing event. This may depend on your team's usual practices and pattern of meetings. It is worth discussing it with your team leader. Teams have a role in learning, keeping abreast of new information, questioning and challenging social work trends in changing times and maximising developments.

Effective teams are supportive, give team members power and build strength through sharing experiences and collective action. You may be a member of other groups and teams – your family, neighbourhood association, leisure centre or sport team. You may be able to draw on experiences related to your participation in faith groups or religious affiliation, adult education, school parents' associations and other local groups. All these and more may mean you can bring transferable skills to your work team and find ways to strengthen it.

Activity: Characteristics of good teams

To some extent, measuring a good or effective team will involve subjective elements. What some team members enjoy and receive from a team will differ from others. Below are some measures you can consider and discuss with other members of your team. The exercise will help you measure you team's effectiveness and provide you with a tool to discuss what constitutes success within a team.

Positive team characteristics	Your comments on their achievement or need to develop them further
Low staff/membership turnover	
No (or few) vacancies	
Vacancies quickly filled due to applications from suitable candidates	
No (or low) absenteeism	
An appropriate mix/balance of roles, diversity and expertise	
Regular team meetings	
Good attendance at team meetings	
A satisfactory mixture of meetings and agendas (business, planning, case discussions, topics, team development)	
Constructive meetings with debate but no animosity	
Team members happy with how decisions are made	
Positive relationships	
Mutual help and support evident	
Conflicts managed and resolved	
Healthy informal communication	
More face-to-face communication than emails and written information	
Lively flow of ideas	
Good internal networking	
Good networking with other agencies and professionals	
Optimism about the future	
Appropriate informal and social gatherings	
The team is known and regarded positively within the organisation	

(Continued)

Activity *Continued*

Positive team characteristics	*Your comments on their achievement or need to develop them further*
Achieving goals and targets	
Successfully accomplishing team tasks	
Good morale	
Team members express personal and professional satisfaction with the team	

As part of introducing the book, Chapter 1 highlighted that merely reading it would not make you an accomplished team worker or result in you suddenly having excellent teamworking skills. Perhaps through reflection and completing the activities you have been able to interact with the ideas in the book beyond passive reading.

This book will have achieved another of its aims if it has stimulated your thinking and encouraged you to undertake some of the further reading suggested at the end of each chapter. All social workers are expected to engage in continuous professional development (CPD) and it is far more productive and meaningful if you do this because you genuinely wish to progress professionally rather than as a duty or chore to be ticked off a list of requirements. Continuous professional development is furthered through your own informal personal learning and researching topics as well as attendance at training events and courses. Engaging in activities as part of your work, such as those listed in the bullet points above, can also be part of CPD.

Continuous professional development includes the development of professional skills but you need to consider and plan ways of doing this. A skill, like riding a bicycle, typing or word processing, can be learnt, improved and developed. However, in cycling and typing there are more precise, observable end products that evidence your skill level. Professional skills generally and teamworking skills more specifically are more difficult to pin down and evidence due to their multifaceted and complex nature, as stated at the beginning of this chapter.

A starting point in developing teamworking skills is an honest self-assessment of your skills set. Using tools in this textbook may help you, particularly the skills checklist in Chapter 5. Continuous development of skills requires ongoing self-awareness. It is important to ask for feedback and discuss your skills openly with others. You will benefit from exploring ways of obtaining feedback from fellow team members, from service users and carers and from your line manager, including through formal appraisals. Skills related to receiving and giving feedback themselves are part of teamworking.

You may have come across the Johari window diagram. It is named after Joe Luft and Harry Ingram (1955) who first proposed the model of interpersonal awareness presented in Figure 10.1. The window depicts aspects of ourselves that we make public

	Known to self	Not known to self
Known to others	**OPEN ARENA**	**LACK OF SELF-AWARENESS**
Not known to others	**CLOSED GUARDED FACADE**	**UNCONSCIOUS PROCESSES UNKNOWN AREAS YET TO EMERGE**

Figure 10.1

and those that we keep to ourselves, against the extent to which others get to know us. The four window 'panes' are relevant to skills development. Adult-to-Adult, honest communication keeps us in the open arena with a good measure of self-awareness (known to self) and others knowing us well (known to others). Individuals who are appropriately open about themselves tend to be good team workers.

To minimise those personal behaviours and traits of which we may not be aware (not known to self) but that others notice and know about us (known to others), we need to solicit feedback to increase our self-awareness. There may be skills that we don't have or perform rather poorly. If others observe this and tell us, we can improve. There may also be skills we are good at without us realising it, so positive feedback from others can boost our self-esteem.

Being closed and guarded probably using defence mechanisms and putting on a personal or professional facade does not make us good team workers. Effective team-working involves being open about ourselves and sharing information as part of healthy communication. Appropriate self-disclosure is part of teamworking and encourages others to reciprocate. It is easier to do this when there is trust within a team.

Aspects of ourselves not known to us and that are not known to others either may be unconscious processes or unknown new awareness and professional development areas yet to emerge. To develop skills you need to seek feedback, build self-awareness, challenge and surprise yourself by catching yourself behaving differently.

Finally, you could consider the application of CPD to your team, as well as to you individually. As already suggested, finding ways of sharing your knowledge and current experience will also benefit the team. All activities in this book lend themselves to discussion within your team. Why not have a go?

References

Adair, J. (1973) *Action-centred Leadership*. London: McGraw-Hill.

Adair, J. (1986) *Effective Teambuilding*. London: Gower Publishing.

Andersen, S.M., Glassman, N.S., Chen, S. and Cole, S.W. (1995) Transference in social perception: the role of chronic accessibility in significant-other representations, *Journal of Personality and Social Psychology*, 69, 41–57.

Bailey, D. and Liyanage, L. (2012) The role of the mental health social worker: political pawns in the reconfiguration of adult health and social care, *British Journal of Social Work*, 42(6), 1113–31.

Bayliss, J. (2009) *Working in a Team: A Workbook to Successful Dynamics*. London: MA Healthcare.

Belbin, R.M. (1991) *Management Teams: Why They Succeed or Fail*. Oxford: Butterworth-Heinemann.

Belbin, R.M. (2000) *Beyond the Team*. Oxford: Butterworth-Heinemann.

Belbin, R.M. (2010) *Team Roles at Work*, 2nd edn. Oxford: Butterworth-Heinemann.

Benson, J. (2010) *Working More Creatively with Groups*, 3rd edn. Abingdon: Routledge.

Berne, E. (1973) *Games People Play: The Psychology of Human Relationships*. London: Penguin Books.

Brewin, C.R. and Andrews, B. (2000) Psychological defence mechanisms: the example of repression, *The Psychologist*, 13(12), 615–17.

BASW (British Association of Social Workers) (2010) *BASW Policy on Social Work in Multi Disciplinary Mental Health Teams*. Birmingham: BASW.

Cheminais, R. (2009) *Effective Multi-Agency Partnerships: Putting Every Child Matters into Practice*. London: Sage.

Commons Health Select Committee (2011) *Written Evidence from the NHS Confederation (SC 74)*. Available at: http://www.publications.parliament.uk/pa/cm201012/cmselect/cmhealth/1583/1583we19.htm [accessed 1 August 2012].

Crawford, K. (2012) *Interprofessional Collaboration in Social Work Practice*. London: Sage.

Daley, G. (1989) Professional ideology or organisational tribalism?, in R. Taylor and J. Ford (eds.) *Social Work and Health Care*. London: Jessica Kingsley.

D'Andrade, R. (1990) Some propositions about the relations between culture and human cognition, in J. Stigler, R. Shweder and G. Herdt (eds.) *Cultural Psychology – Essays on Comparative Human Development*. Cambridge: Cambridge University Press.

Deutsch, M., Coleman, P. and Marcus, E. (eds.) (2006) *The Handbook of Conflict Resolution: Theory and Practice*. San Francisco, CA: Wiley.

Edwards, D. (1996) *Discourse and Cognition*. London: Sage.

Glasby, J. (2012) *'We have to stop meeting like this': what works in health and local government partnerships?* Policy Paper #13. Birmingham: University of Birmingham, Health Services Management Centre, Institute of Local Government Studies.

Graham, M. (2002) *Social Work and African-centred Worldviews*. London: Venture Press.

Granville, J. and Langton, P. (2002) Working across boundaries: systemic and psycho-dynamic perspectives on multidisciplinary and inter-agency practice, *Journal of Social Work Practice*, 16(1), 23–7.

Gushue, G. and Constantine, M. (2003) Examining individualism, collectivism, and self-differentiation in African American college women, *Journal of Mental Health Counseling*, 25(1), 1–16.

Hafford-Letchfield, T. (2009) *Management and Organisations in Social Work*, 2nd edn. Exeter: Learning Matters.

Hardingham, A. and Royal, J. (1994) *Pulling Together: Teamwork in Practice*. London: Institute of Personnel and Development.

Hargie, O. and Dickson, D. (2004) *Skilled Interpersonal Communication: Research, Theory and Practice*. Hove: Routledge.

Helm, D. (2010) *Making Sense of Child and Family Assessment: How to Interpret Children's Needs*. London: Jessica Kingsley.

Howe, D. (2008) *The Emotionally Intelligent Social Worker*. Basingstoke: Palgrave Macmillan.

Hudson, B. (2002) Interprofessionality in health and social care: the Achilles' heel of partner-ship?, *Journal of Interprofessional Care*, 16(1), 7–17.

Hughes, M. and Wearing, M. (2007) *Organisations and Management in Social Work*, 2nd edn. London: Sage.

Janis, I. (1972) *Victims of Groupthink*. New York: Houghton Mifflin.

Kadushin, A. and Harkness, D. (2002) *Supervision in Social Work*, 4th edn. New York: Columbia University Press.

Karpman, S. (1968) Fairy tales and script drama analysis, *Transactional Analysis Bulletin*, 7(26), 39–43.

Laming, H. (2003) *The Victoria Climbié Inquiry Report*. Cm 5730. London: The Stationery Office.

Lencioni, P. (2005) *Overcoming the Five Dysfunctions of a Team: A Field Guide for Leaders, Managers and Facilitators*. San Francisco, CA: Jossey-Bass.

Levi, D. (2007) *Group Dynamics for Teams*, 2nd edn. Thousand Oaks, CA: Sage.

Lippmann, W. (1922) *Public Opinion*. New York: Free Press.

Lomax, R., Jones, K., Leigh, S. and Gay, C. (2010) *Surviving Your Social Work Placement*. Basingstoke: Palgrave Macmillan.

Loughran, H., Hohman, M. and Finnegan, D. (2010) Predictors of role legitimacy and role adequacy of social workers working with substance-using clients, *British Journal of Social Work*, 40(1), 239–56.

Luft, J. and Ingram, H. (1955) The Johari window, a graphic model of interpersonal aware-ness. *Proceedings of the Western Training Laboratory in Group Development*. Los Angeles, CA: University of California.

Lymbery, M. and Butler, S. (2004) *Social Work Ideals and Practice Realities*. Basingstoke: Palgrave Macmillan.

Maginn, M. (2004) *Making Teams Work: 24 Lessons for Working Together Successfully*. New York: McGraw-Hill.

Martin, R. (2010) *Social Work Assessment*. Exeter: Learning Matters.

Maslow, A. (1954) *Motivation and Personality*. New York: Harper.

Melin Emilsson, U. (2011) The role of social work in cross-professional teamwork: examples from an older people's team in England, *British Journal of Social Work*. DOI: 10.1093/bjsw/bcr185.

Morris, K. (ed.) (2008) *Social Work and Multi-agency Working: Making a Difference*. Bristol: The Policy Press.

Morrison, T. (2007) Emotional intelligence, emotion and social work: context, characteristics, complications and contribution, *British Journal of Social Work*, 37(2), 245–63.

Munro, E. (2011) *The Munro Review of Child Protection: Final Report, A Child-centred System*. Cm 8062. Norwich: The Stationery Office.

Neck, C. and Manz, C. (2012) *Mastering Self-leadership: Empowering Yourself for Personal Excellence*, 6th edn. Englewood Cliffs, NJ: Prentice-Hall.

Nolan, M. (1995) Towards an ethos of interdisciplinary practice, *British Medical Journal*, 312, 305–6.

Onyett, S. (2003) *Teamworking in Mental Health*. Basingstoke: Palgrave Macmillan.

Øvretveit, J. (1995) Team decision-making, *Journal of Interprofessional Care*, 9(1), 41–51.

Oxford Dictionary (2012) *Oxford Dictionaries on line*. Available at: http://oxforddictionaries.com/ [accessed 13 September 2012].

Payne, M. (2000) *Teamwork in Multiprofessional Care*. Basingstoke: Palgrave Macmillan.

Pirrie, A., Wilson, V., Elsegood, J., Hall, J., Hamilton, S., Harden, R., Lee, D. and Stead, J. (1998) *Evaluating Multidisciplinary Education in Health Care*. Edinburgh: SCRE.

Power, M.J. (1997) Conscious and unconscious representations of meaning, in M.J. Power and C.R. Brewin (eds.) *The Transformation of Meaning in Psychological Therapies*. Chichester: Wiley.

Pugh, G., Dame (2007) Foreword, in I. Siraj-Blatchford, K. Clarke and M. Needham, *The Team Around the Child: Multi-agency Working in the Early Years*. Stoke-on-Trent: Trentham Books.

Ritchie, J., Dick, D. and Lingham, R. (1994) *The Report of the Inquiry into the Care and Treatment of Christopher Clunis*. London: The Stationery Office.

Rogers, C. (1961) *On Becoming a Person: A Therapist's View of Psychotherapy*. London: Constable.

Salovey, P. and Mayer, J. (1990) Emotional intelligence, *Imagination, Cognition and Personality*, 9, 185–211.

Schiller, L. (2003) Women's group development from a relational model and a new look at facilitator influence on group development, in M. Cohen and A. Mullender (eds.) *Gender and Groupwork*. New York: Routledge.

Senge, P. (1990) *The Fifth Discipline: The Art and Practice of the Learning Organization*. New York: Doubleday.

Sharkey, P. (2007) *The Essentials of Community Care*, 2nd edn. Basingstoke: Palgrave Macmillan.

Siraj-Blatchford, I., Clarke, K. and Needham, M. (2007) *The Team Around the Child: Multi-agency Working in the Early Years*. Stoke-on-Trent: Trentham Books.

SWRB (Social Work Reform Board) (2010) *Building a Safe and Confident Future: One Year On. Proposed Standards for Employers of Social Workers in England and Proposed Supervision Framework*. London: SWRB.

The College of Social Work (2012) *Professional Capabilities Framework*. Available at: http://www.collegeofsocialwork.org/pcf.aspx [accessed 22 September 2012].

Thomas, K. (2002) *Thomas-Kilmann Conflict Mode Instrument*. Menlo Park, CA: CPP, Inc.

Thompson, N. (2009) *People Skills*, 3rd edn. Basingstoke: Palgrave Macmillan.

Thylefors, I., Persson, O. and Hellström, D. (2005) Team types, perceived efficiency and team climate in Swedish crossprofessional teamwork, *Journal of Interprofessional Care*, 19(2), 102–14.

Trevithick, P. (2012) *Social Work Skills and Knowledge: A Practice Handbook*. Maidenhead: Open University Press.

Tsui, M. (2005) *Social Work Supervision: Contexts and Concepts*. Thousand Oaks, CA: Sage.

Tuckman, B. (1965) Developmental sequence in small groups, *Psychological Bulletin*, 63, 384–99.

Vogt, L. and Laher, S. (2009) The five factor model of personality and individualism/collectivism in South Africa: an exploratory study, *Psychology in Society*, 37, 39–54.

Walker, H. (2008) *Studying for Your Social Work Degree*. Exeter: Learning Matters.

Wilson, V. and Pirrie, A. (2000) *Multidisciplinary Teamworking: Beyond the Barriers? A Review of the Issues*. SCRE Research Report #96. Glasgow: SCRE.

Woodcock, M. (1989) *Team Development Manual*, 2nd edn. Aldershot: Gower.

Wright, P., Turner, C., Clay, D. and Mills, H. (2006) *The Participation of Children and Young People in Developing Social Care*. London: SCIE.

Index

A page number in **bold** denotes the reference is in a table or checklist

Absenteeism, no (or low), as a characteristic
    of good teams **117**
Accommodating, as an orientation towards
    conflict 31–2, 37
Accomplishment(s)
    of team tasks, as a characteristic of good
        teams **118**
    team 21, 28, 29, 40, 104
Accountability
    line management 76
    networks 70
    Serious Case Reviews' (SCR) 73
    team 68, 74
    team leader's 44
    to the team from support staff 47
    unclear 91
    see also Liability; Responsibility
Achievement
    as part of defining a team 10, 23
    individual 4, 45, 49
    of goals and targets, as a characteristic of
        good teams 118
    of team aims, results, task 8, 13, 17, 28,
        33–5, 50, 54, 104
Active listening 27, 37, 53, 56, **62**
Adair, J. 11, 33
Adult-to-Adult
    communication/transactions 16, 24, 45,
        54, 88, 109, 119
    see also Communication

African-centred values 42–3, 104
    see also Collectivism
Allowable weaknesses 41, **41–2**, 42, 45, 110
Assertiveness 37, 55, 60, **62**, 88, 99
Assessment jigsaw 93–4, 100
Attending to others **62**
Avoiding, as an orientation towards conflict
    31–2, 37
    Case example 32

Belbin, R.M. 40, 41, 50, 51, 78
Berne, E. 16, 18
Blame culture
    see Culture, blame
Boundaries
    disciplinary 81, 82
    geographical 95, 96–7, 100, 115
    organisational 100
    personal v. professional 57, 63
    opening 99
    permeable 21–2, 24, 112
    professional 80, 81, 100
    role 99
    team 21–2, **24**, 46–7, 69
British Association of Social Workers
    (BASW) 81–2

Centre for the Advancement of
    Interprofessional Education (CAIPE)
    79

Challenge and change 29, 30, 110
  See also Storming
Challenging other team members 53, **62**
Chaotic teams 22, **24**
  see also Conforming teams; Flexible teams
Characteristics of good teams 116, **117–18**
Circular causality 22
Climbié, Victoria 76, 91, 92, 95
Clunis, Christopher 91, 95
Cognitive behavioural theories 13, 15
  see also Social cognition
Cognitive schema 86
  see also Cultural model
Cognitive script 13
Collaboration
  and interpersonal relationships 54–5, 62
  inter-agency 80, 91
  inter-professional 79, 81, 92, 93, 96–7,
    99–100, 107–8
  Case example 82
  lack of 15, 91
  multi-agency 91, 98, 107
  team 47, 49
Collaborating
  and sharing information 94
  as a student 102, 105
  as an orientation towards conflict 31–3,
    62
  Case example 32–3
  with other professionals 4, 94, 107
  with team colleagues 10, 12, 23, 28, 32,
    34–5, 43, 49, 54–5, 56, 62, 71, 87, 89,
    99
Collaborative mindset 99
Collectivism 104
Colwell, Maria 92
Communication
  Adult-to-Adult 16, 45, 88, 109, 112, 119
  email 53–4, 60, 61, 62, 88, 99, 107, 116,
    117
  Case example 95
  face-to-face v. email and written, as a
    characteristic of good teams 117
  healthy informal, as a characteristic of
    good teams 117

  key to collaboration 99
  skills 53–4, 56, 62, 89, 107
  verbal 57, 62, 70, 89
  written 46, 54, 57, 62, 64, 70, 71, 88, 117
Community of practice 69, 77, 114
  see also Learning organisation
Community Mental Health Teams (CMHTs)
    20, 81, 83
  as matrix teams 69
  as multidisciplinary team 79
  Case example 14–15
Competing, as an orientation towards
    conflict 31–2, 37
Completer finisher (team role) **41**
  Case example 43
  reserved leader 44
Compromising, as an orientation towards
    conflict 31–2, 37
Connexions 79
  as matrix teams 69
Conflict(s) 28, 30, 36–7, 45, 81
  inner 13, 15
  constructive and creative use of 27, 45
  Case example 33
  managed and resolved, as a characteristic
    of good teams 117
  management of 45, 55, 89, 110
  orientations, or responses, towards 31–2,
    37, 55
  see also Accommodating
    Avoiding
    Collaborating
    Competing
    Compromising
Conforming teams 22, **24**, 46
  see also Chaotic teams; Flexible teams
Contexts and Organisations PCF domain 9,
    67, 74, 89, 98
Continuous Professional Development
    (CPD) 118
  applied to the team 119
Coordinator (team role) **41**
  Case example 43
Cooperation 22, 35, 45, 49, 35, 56, 98
in responding to conflict 55, **62**

with other professionals and disciplines 94, 98, 108
Connecting with others 54, **62**
Critical Reflection and Analysis
as teamworking skills 60, **63**
PCF domain 9, 60, 88
Culture
  and language 80, 85–6, 88
  blame 74
  carriers 71
  individual 42, 104
  family 3
  learning 72, 74
organisational 20, 70–1, 72, 73–4, 78
Case examples 43, 73
stereotypes 86, 90
team 4, 8, 12, 46, 47, 70–1, 83, 105
Case examples 83, 108–9
Cultural model 86
  see also Cognitive schema
Debate within a team 53, 54, 55, **62**
  but no animosity, as a characteristic of good teams 117
Decision-making 41, 27, 43, 49, 60–1, **63**, 86
  in leadership 40
  team members happy with , as a characteristic of good teams 117
Defence mechanisms 15, 23, 56, 119
Disclosure, in responding to conflict 55, **62**
  self 119
Disputes, work 26, 36
Disagreement(s) 22, 28, 29, 31, 36–7, 54, **62**, 99, 106, 107, 110
Drama triangle 18–19, 22, 55
Dynamics
  family 21
  group 61, 104
  power 31, 68, 86, 89, 109, 115
  team 11, 12, 17, 18, 22, 26, 31, 36, 45, 46, 102, 112

Ecological theories/approaches 19, 69, 112
Email
  see Communication, email

Emotional intelligence (EI) 7, 36, 47–9, 57, **63**, 73, 110
Emotional resilience 47–9, 50, 57, **63**, 73, 110
Empathy 29, 56, **62**
  lacking 36
Ending
  during the life of a student cohort 104
  stage of team development 27, 29, 30
Engaging with others 54, 55, **62**, 108
Ego state(s) 16–18, 55, 109
Ethical reasoning 56, **63**
Evidence based practice 73

Family dynamics
  see Dynamics, family
Feedback, giving and receiving 27, 34, 53, **62**, 118, 119
Feminist viewpoint 29, 37
  see also Relational model
Flexibility, in responding to conflict 55, **62**
Flexible teams 22, **24**, 46, 99
  see also Chaotic teams; Conforming teams
Forming
  during the life of a student cohort 103
  stage of team development 28, 29
Freud, S. 13
Functional role(s) 40, 45, 79, 80, 104
  team leadership 43, 44, 45
  see also Team role(s)

Game playing in TA 16, 18, 55, 86, 89
Gutting a book 6–7
Group(s)
life, models of 28, 29
organic 27
processes 45, 61, 94, 104
stages 27, 118
student 102, 105, 106–8
Case example 106–7
supervision 76–7, 78
team as a group of people 3, 12, 33, 69, 84–6
see also Groupthink
Group dynamics
  see Dynamics, group

Groupthink 61, **63**, 94
  case example 95

Hackney, London Borough of 78
  Case example 73
Hierarchies, organisational 68, 74
Homeostasis 22, **24**

Ideas
  accepting new members' 46
  disclosure – being open to others' 55
  exploring 45, 53, 105
  listening to individuals' 44
  lively flow of, as a characteristic of good
    teams 117
  low morale due to stifling 45
Implementer (team role) **41**
  Case example 43
Inclusion 27, 82, 86
Individual needs 31, 33–5
  see also Task needs; Team needs
Individualism 104
Interacting with others 16, 54, **62**, 105
Interactions, formula to work out 12
Interdependency
  as part of defining a team 10–11, 23
  in individual relationships 31, 47, 50, 54,
    89, 102, 105
  relating to size of team 11–12
  systemic 19
  team 28, 35, 43, 49, 106
  within different professional disciplines 82
Interdisciplinary teams/work 20, 55, 77,
    80–1
Interpersonal intelligence 48
Interpersonal relationships/transactions 16,
    18, 22, 54–5, **62**, 89, 100
Inter-professional
  working 57, 80–1, 94, 99
  collaboration 55, 81, 93, 99, 108
  inadequate/poor 92, 95–7
Interruptions, managing 53, 59–60, **63**
Intrapersonal intelligence 48

Johari window 118–19

Key worker, appointment of 94, 96, 99
  see also Lead professional
Knowledge
  of your organisation 57, 63, 67
  of your role 74
  PCF domain 9

Lead professional, appointment of 94, 99
  see also Key worker
Leadership
  as a functional role 40, 43, 45
  as a team role 8, 21, 40, 45, 71
  styles 22, 40, 44
  see also Team leader(ship)
Learning organisation 69, 72, 74, 114
  see also Community of practice
Liability, determining 73, 74
  see also Accountability; Responsibility
Life of teams 26–7
Line management 47, 68, 76
Link pin structure 68, 74

Macro level/context 20, 22, **24**, 49, 57, **63**,
    72, 78, 81, 112
Maintenance needs 32–5, 37
  See also Team needs
Managerialism 20, 68, 73
Maslow, A 4
Matrix structures/teams 68, 69
  Case example 75
Mediation 36–7
Meeting(s)
  and agendas mix (business, planning,
    case discussions, topics, team
    development), as a characteristic of
    good teams 117
  chairing 45, 63
  contributing agenda items 63
  constructive, as a characteristic of good
    teams 117
  good attendance, as a characteristic of
    good teams 117
  participating in 61, 63, 89
  regular, as a characteristic of good teams
    117

taking minutes 40, 45
team 28–9, 31, 34, 35, 47, 53, 68, 71, 86,
    106–7, 116, 117
Case examples 32–3, 43
Meso level/context 20–1, 22, **24**, 57, **63**, 72,
    78, 112
Metadiscipline 80, 84
    see also Trans-professional
Micro level 20, 21, **24**, 49, 72, 81, 112
Monitor evaluator (team role) **41**
    Case example 43
Morale
    as part of team culture 70
    good, as a characteristic of good teams
        118
    low, 35
    strong team 34, 45, 57
    Case example 43
Multidisciplinary working
    application of systemic and
        psychodynamic perspectives to
        22–3
    Case example 73
    skills 87–8
    teams/practice 77, 79–81, 82, 83, 84, 85,
        86
    Case example 83
Munro, Prof E. report 20, 72–3, 92, 94, 96
Mutual help and support, as a characteristic
    of good teams **117**

Network(s)
    as part of socially constructed reality 20
    in relation to the permeability of teams
        21, 22
    approaches 68, 69
    Case example 75
    within organisations 70
Networking
    good internal, as a characteristic of good
        teams 117
    skills 62, 69, 89, 99, 100
    to build a team around the service user 55
    with other agencies and professionals, as
        a characteristic of good teams 117

New team members
    support for, as part of meeting individual
        needs 35
    implications for team 46, 71
Non-verbal communication/responses
    as part of defining team boundaries
        21
    importance of 53, 55–6, 62
    as part of interaction and collaboration
        with team colleagues 89
Norming
    during the life of a student cohort 103
    stage of team development 28, 29

Objectivity 16, 48, 54, 55, 57, **62**, 107
    male stereotype 42
    v. emotions 36, 48
Open
    communication/relationships 16–17, 23,
        28, 31, 45, 46, 47, 49, 53, 56, 71, 86,
        89, 97, 107, 119
    teamwork 21
Optimism about the future, as a
        characteristic of good teams **117**
Orientation to conflict 31
    see also Conflict, responding to
Organisational
    culture 70–1, 72, 86
    differences and boundaries 100
    frameworks/policy 54, 57, 67, 68, 74
    procedures 35
structure(s) 20, 40, 47, 68, 70, 74–5, 99
systems 98
tribalism 80, 97
see also Tribal allegiances

Participation
    in meetings 61, 63
in responding to conflict 55, **62**
Partnership
    promoting 56, 63
    skills 52
    working in 20, 79, 94. 98, 103
People who use services 4, 8, 71, 87
    See also Service users and carers

Performing
during the life of a student cohort
103–4
stage of team development 27, 28, 29, 30,
34
Permeable boundaries
see Boundaries, permeable
Persecutor
role 18–19, 110
Case example 32
see also Rescuer; Victim
Personal organisational skills 57–60, **63**
Placement
experience 108–10
with the team 108
see also Practice placement opportunities
Planning
inadequate 91
skills/techniques 61, 63
Plant (team role) **41**
Case example 43
Positive belief system **24**
Power
imbalance 36
issues 27, 30–1
misuse 55
relationship(s) 17, 74
struggles 100, 106
Power dynamics
see Dynamics, power
Practice learning opportunities 108–10
see also Placement experience
Prioritising 58, 60, 61, **63**
Problem-solving 27, 60, **63**, 89
Professional Capabilities Framework
(PCF) 8–9, 20, 21,52, 56, 57, 60, 67,
74, 88, 89, 98, 99
Professional
boundaries 57, 63, 80, 97
demeanour 63
mindset and attitude 98–9
practice skills 88
principles 32
role boundaries 81
values/value base 4, 8, 56, 70, 71

Professionalism
PCF domain 9, 57, 98, 99
skills 56–7, **63**, 88
Psychodynamic approaches/theory 13–16,
22–3

Reclaiming Social Work programme 78
Case example 73
Relational model 29–30
See also Feminist viewpoint
Relationships
and responding to conflict 31
developing, in placement 108
factors affecting 13
formula to work out 12
interpersonal 22, 54–5, 62, 89, 100
positive 35, 117 (as a characteristic of
good teams)
power 74
working/professional 16–19, 36–7
Reliability 57, **63**, 98
Rescuer
role 18–19
Case example 32
see also Persecutor; Victim
Resource investigator (team role) **41**
Case example 43
outgoing leader 44
Responsibility
diffusion of 94, 95, 99
link-pin 68
of all team members 35, 61, 80
personal 74, 83, 88, 99, 104–5
self 60
team leader/manager 35, 44
see also Accountability; Liability
see also Groupthink
Restructuring, organisational 20, 68, 98,
99
Risk (and concerns) assessment/
management **63**, 94, 97, 60, 100
Role
adequacy 82–3, 90
clarity of 99
legitimacy 82–3, 90

Roles, diversity, expertise mix/balance, as a characteristic of good teams **117**

Rogers, C 56

Rogerian qualities 56

Satisfaction
  sense of 4, 35
  team members' personal and professional, as a characteristic of good teams 118
Self-assessment 114, 118
Self-awareness 30, 36, 43, 48, 49, 56, **63**, 87, 119
Self-congruence 56, **63**, 87
Self leadership 49–50, 88
Self-management 36, 48, 49, 57–60, **63**, 87–8
Serious Case Reviews (SCRs) 72–3
Service users and carers
  as members of a multidisciplinary team 87
  involvement and participation 8, 71, 77, 87, 89
  Case example 43
  see also People who use services; Whole systems approach
Shaper (team role) **41**
  Case example 43
Size of teams 11–12, **23**, 34, 80
Social cognition 14
  see also Cognitive behavioural theories
Social events/informal gatherings 34, 45, 47, 49
  as a characteristic of good teams 117
Social Work Reform Board 20, 88
Social Work Taskforce 20
Socially constructed reality 20, 22
Specialist (team role) **41**
  Case example 43
Sport team analogies 11, 54–5
Stages of team development 28–9
  as a student cohort 103–4

  see also Ending
  Forming
  Norming
  Performing
  Storming
Stereotypes/Stereotyping 42, 84–6, 90, 97
  avoiding 100
  challenging stereotypical thinking 89
Storming
  during the life of a student cohort 103
  stage of team development 28, 29, 30, 31, 110
  Case example 32
  see also Challenge and change
Stress management 48, 49, 60, **63**, 88
Student experience
  assessment concerns 110
  collaboration 102
  informal teamwork 105–7
  interdependence 102
  personal and cultural factors 104–5
  small group work 106–7
  Case example 106
Supervision
  as a student 108
  Case example 108–9
  as part of meeting individual needs 35
  as part of meeting task needs 33
  from another professional 89
models of 75–7
Case example 75
  seeking it as part of professional practice 88
SWOT analysis 60
Synergy 12, **23**, 26, 40, 61, 80, 82
Systems/systemic
  analysis/perspectives 22–3, 99, 114
  approaches 68, 69, 77, 78, 99
  theory 19–21, 72, 77

Task needs 33–5, 37
  see also Individual needs; Team needs
Team(s)
  as systems 21

boundaries 21–2
definition of 10–11, 24
in organisations 68
is known and regarded positively within
    the organisation, as a characteristic of
    good teams 117
membership 45, 50
name 11, 23
player 89
resilience 49, 50
    supervision 77
    working as a single unit 11, 23
    see also Chaotic; Conforming; Flexible
Team culture
    see Culture, team
Team dynamics
    see Dynamics, team
Team around the child (TAC) 93
Team around the service user 92–3, 97, 99
Team leader(ship) 21, 29, 43–4, 50, 76
    see also Leadership styles
Team meetings
    see Meetings, team
Team needs 33–5, 37
    see also Individual needs; Maintenance
        needs; Task needs
Team roles 40–2, 50, 104
    see also Functional roles
Team Role theory 40, 45
Teamworker (team role) **41**
    Case example 43
Time management 58, 60, **63**
Transactional Analysis (TA) 16–18, 55, 112
Transference 14, 23, 56
    Case example 14–15
Trans-professional 81
    see also Metadiscipline

Tribal allegiances 80, 97
    See also Organisational tribalism
Tuckman, B 28, 30
Turnover, low
    as a characteristic of good teams 117

Unconditional positive regard 56, **62**
Unconscious processes 13–14, 15, 56, 119
    Case example 14–15

Vacancies
    low or few, as a characteristic of good
        teams 117
    unfilled 47
    quickly filled, as characteristic of good
        teams 117
Values and ethics
    PCF domain 9, 56
in teamworking 56
see also Professional values
Verbal communication
    see Communication, verbal
Victim
    role 18–19, 110
    case example 32
    see also Persecutor; Rescuer

Whole systems approach 71–2, 78
    Case example 73
Workload management 34, 58, 60, **63**

Youth Offending Team(s) (YOTs)
    as matrix teams 69
    as multidisciplinary teams 20, 79–80
    Case examples 69–70, 83–4, 108–9

Zito, Jonathan 91